The Still Point

And the

Dance

STILL POINT

'At the still point of the turning world. Neither flesh nor fleshless;
Neither from nor towards; at the still point, there the dance is,
But neither arrest nor movement. And do not call it fixity,
Where past and future are gathered. Neither movement from nor towards,
Neither ascent nor decline. Except for the point, the still point,
There would be no dance, and there is only the dance.'

- TS Eliot

Illness is the dance of symptoms around the still point of health

The Still Point
and the
Dance

Healing With Life Force

John Boulderstone

STILL POINT

Please read:

I, John Boulderstone, am the author of this book and wish to make clear that I am not a doctor, I have never been a doctor and I do not want to be a doctor. Nor do I claim to be a Western healthcare professional.

The information in this book is based on my personal opinions, experiences and research and might challenge conventional thinking. I have nearly forty years' clinical experience as an alternative healthcare practitioner. Western medicine is where it is for a reason. Understand that reason by getting professional Western medical advice. Always consult with relevant professionals before making significant changes.

The information in this book is not intended as a prescription for any disease. I wouldn't and couldn't put myself in the position of advising you about your personal health issues through the medium of a book. You are unique and your history, which I do not know, is what has brought you to this point.

You are responsible for your own health and I encourage you to research, question and seek information from trusted sources before making any changes to your health practices. Trusted sources do not include people who are currently being bribed by the pharmaceutical industry.

I only want happiness for you. Only make changes to your life after checking with the people that know. All I know is emptiness and nothingness and the difference between them.

By reading this book, you acknowledge that you are responsible for your own health decisions and will consult with qualified professionals as needed.

Contents

APPENDIX

Introduction

This book doesn't merely describe an 'alternative' health system—it outlines a foundational understanding of health itself. You won't find a catalog of remedies for silencing symptoms, as I believe symptoms are our body's way of communicating vital needs. Instead, you'll discover the true origins of illness and a path towards genuine healing.

By learning to listen to our bodies and respond to their needs, we unlock the keys to lasting health and well-being. Ignoring this wisdom has led us to a crisis of escalating healthcare costs, increasingly complex diseases, and a dearth of cures. This book offers a different path, one where we partner with our bodies to achieve optimal health.

Many people instinctively react to their body's warning signals by seeking to suppress them with medicine. The logic seems simple: no signal equals no problem. However, those signals are vital clues to restoring health.

Consider a high fever: it's a sign the body is actively fighting an illness. Artificially lowering the temperature doesn't cure the underlying issue. In fact, it can be counterproductive. Research shows that each 1-degree Fahrenheit rise in temperature doubles the body's metabolic rate, accelerating the elimination of the illness and potentially halving its duration.

Embracing these signals as allies, rather than adversaries, is key to unlocking a path towards genuine healing.

My quest for well-being and inner peace began at the age of 21, during my university years, when I recognised a lack of control over my thoughts. They would often leave me feeling overwhelmed and fearful for my sanity. In response, I turned to daily meditation.

After two decades of dedicated practice, I developed a profound understanding of the concept of life force – the vital energy that flows within us and connects us to the world. I discovered an intuitive ability to sense disruptions in this flow within others. Over the next ten years, I honed this skill, learning how to guide individuals towards clearing these blockages and facilitating their healing journey.

This practice became a window into the true nature of illness, revealing its root causes. By reaching a state of inner stillness, a 'still point', I gained understanding into the essence of health and the roles played by viruses, medicine, and doctors. These understandings are what I share in this book.

But here's the remarkable part: you don't need thirty years of meditation to access this wisdom. In fact, you can learn the entire technique in a matter of minutes.

After completing my university studies, I embarked on a career as a teacher, eventually transitioning into the fields of homeopathy and CranioSacral therapy. Through my experiences in these modalities, I began to develop a deeper understanding of health that diverged from conventional wisdom.

This led me to dedicate my time, resources, and passion to creating a unique healing approach known as the Boulderstone Technique. In 2011, I shared this knowledge in my book, 'Living with Vitality'. Now, over a decade later, this new book represents a significant evolution, offering solutions to a wider range of health challenges.

I sincerely hope this updated work proves to be a valuable resource for you on your journey towards greater well-being.

While this book represents the culmination of my

personal journey, it wouldn't exist without the support and guidance of countless individuals. My wife, Katharine, deserves special recognition for her unwavering encouragement and invaluable contributions. Her presence has been instrumental in bringing this work to life. For a more comprehensive list of those who have played a role, please refer to the Acknowledgements section at the end of the book.

Now, let the dance begin.

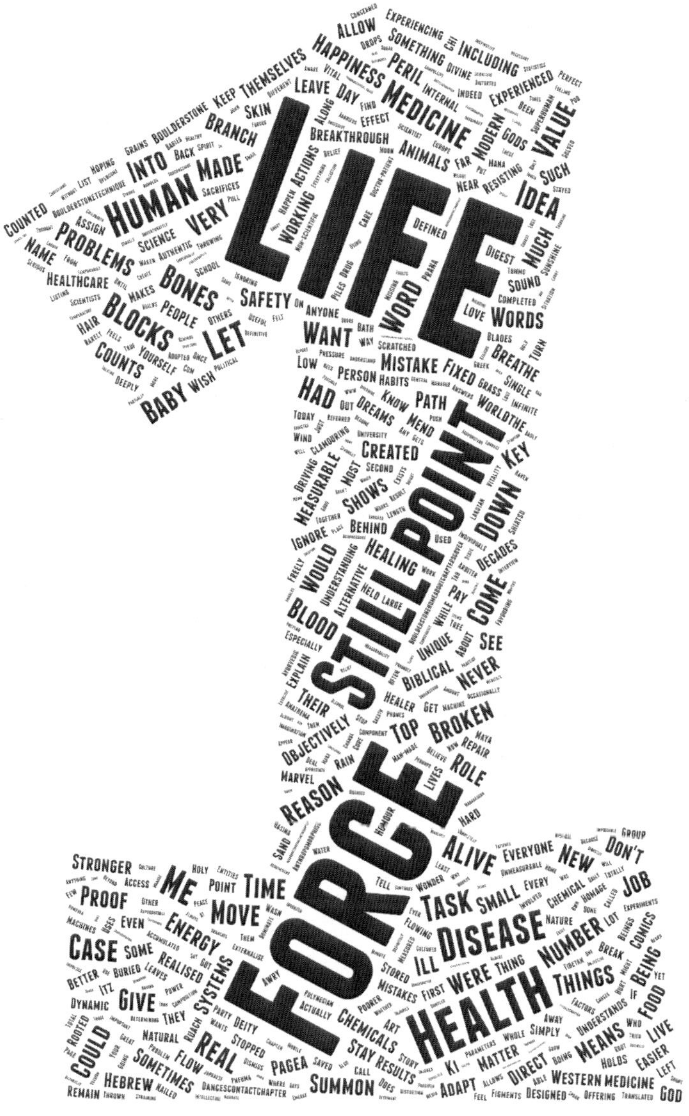

Chapter 1: Life force

The role of the life force

After decades of working in alternative healthcare, I have realised the most direct way to health is to allow the body to heal itself by removing the obstacles that are put in its path. No small job, especially as modern life seems to be clamouring to create new barriers. Removing these obstacles results in a unique state, a still point. The still point is our natural state when the dance of symptoms has stopped. While it may sound like the still point is a fixed state, it isn't; it is dynamic, it is being in the flow of life, in the zone.

The power we all have that allows us to heal ourselves, grow, change and adapt is called the life force. You can ignore it if you wish; many do, but you do so at your peril. While an understanding of the life force seems to have been lost from Western medicine, that doesn't mean it has to be lost to you. The key to health is experiencing the still point and understanding how we put up barriers to the life force. When you don't understand how the life force flows through you, it is easier to make mistakes and by resisting its flow make yourself ill. When you understand how the life force works, you can use it to be authentic, happy, fulfil your dreams and leave all illness behind, such is its power.

Every person who understands the flow of life force in themselves can be their own healer. This book is designed to explain how the life force works, how the still point works, how our actions create illness and how to stay in the zone and be healthy.

Life force exists in every culture

Every culture has its own name for the life force, from

biblical Hebrew to Marvel comics. Feeling the flow of life force and its effect every day is the single most important thing anyone can do to remain healthy and happy.

The life force is defined, simply, as the power and driving force of all animals, including human beings, to stay alive. It is what makes us grow, change our habits, repair our skin when scratched, mend our bones when broken, to digest our food, grow our hair. In other words it allows us to live. You can see why some people assign a deity to the life force, and while some people do, it actually holds us back. It is better to hold our own internal idea about whether the life force is divine or not and keep that idea to ourselves. But the life force can't be accumulated and stored so that people with a large amount become superhuman. We all have access to the same amount but we put up barriers to it and those barriers cause us problems.

And while the life force can't be measured by machines, we all know what it feels like when we can't summon the energy to fulfil a task, when our life force feels low. And we all know what it feels like to summon some deeply buried energy to get a hard task completed. In the first case we have put blocks up to our life force and in the second we have managed to break down the blocks to our life force and use its power. Our life force exists whether we are aware of it or not.

We also know what it is like to have a good day when the life force is flowing freely. No wonder some people want to anthropomorphise it, turn it into a God, pay homage to it and externalise it, hoping that by offering it sacrifices they can get more good days. This is what human beings do, but when they do it it allows others to dismiss these gods as figments of the imagination, even when they are rooted in something real.

Nature, with its near infinite number of leaves or blades of grass or grains of sand or perfect sunshine or drops of rain, has life force running through it and when we become one with the life force, we move to a still point. This is an anathema to the scientist who wants everything nailed down. The life force also exists in man-made entities like a political party, a school or university, or any group of individuals that come together for the same reason.

Unfortunately, as far as Western medicine is concerned, there is a problem with life force. The life force is unmeasurable by science and when Western medicine adopted science and reproducible experiments as the arbiter of what was useful and what wasn't, there was no place left for the unmeasurable life force.

Just because it can't be objectively measured doesn't mean it isn't useful. Many things in life can't be measured that are useful including happiness, love, humour, art and all of them have a life force component. Without them we would be so much poorer. Throwing them away because they can't be measured would be a mistake.

Not everything that counts can be counted, and not everything that can be counted counts - Einstein

Science and measurability have been held up as the most important factors in determining what is real but that has, occasionally, been a mistake. When human beings are involved, science is useful but it doesn't hold all the answers or tell the whole story.

This move to 'science' made Western medicine into the great machine it is today and saved a lot of lives while doing so. But, in favouring science, statistics and measurable parameters, Western Medicine lost something important along the way.

The life force isn't measurable in the way that temperature, blood pressure and blood composition are. Even so, every culture has a word for it. Indeed, even Western Medicine does but it is rarely used in a doctor-patient interview and its value isn't totally understood; that word is vitality. In biblical Hebrew it is called Ruach and sometimes referred to as wind or breath; in acupuncture, shiatsu and acupressure it is called Chi. In Ayurvedic medicine it is called Prana and often translated as breath but it still means life force. The Japanese use Ki, Tibetan Tummo, Madagascan Hasina, Greek Pneuma, Polynesian Mana, Maya Itz, Lakotan Waken, Europe uses Life or Vital Force, and Christians call it Holy Spirit. So it goes on; this is by no means a definitive list.

I appreciate that listing a number of words from different cultures isn't proof of anything. Western medicine is only one branch in a tree of health systems but what value is there in this one branch ignoring something that all the other branches find central to their health systems? Perhaps it had to be done to let science completely dominate but something is going awry with pharmaceutical-based health care. Could it be that Western medicine has thrown out the baby with the non-scientific bath water?

Belief isn't a requirement

It isn't necessary to believe in the life force to be healthy. I work with patients who don't know what the life force is, don't believe in life force or haven't even thought about it. The life force isn't something you have to believe in. However, if you have stayed in a place of happiness and peace for any length of time you have most definitely worked with and been at least partially aware of your life force even if this was instinctive or subconscious. It might sometimes appear to be mystical, after all, it is objectively unmeasurable. This situation reminds me of how imaginary numbers were once thought impossible yet solved complex problems and as a result mobile phones were invented and people got to the moon.

Even with babies and animals who have no intellectual understanding of the life force, it still flows and its flow can still get distorted and that distortion can be felt. Life force may be beyond total comprehension but that doesn't stop me, or you, from feeling where it is distorted in its flow and so be able to do something about it.

Feeling the life force

The way we can all feel the life force most strongly is to just hold our breath. Most people, without practice, can only manage to do that for a minute or so because the life force, the force that wants us to breathe, feels like it gets stronger and stronger, builds up and up, until it forces us to breathe. This also shows that it is possible to overcome the life force for a short amount of time. We temporarily overcome the life force when we are badly hurt and need a place of safety, or are emotionally shocked but say we are alright, or injured and for some reason need to pretend we aren't. Most of us have heard of people who have had serious injuries, even broken bones, but have managed to get home to safety.

Of course the life force shows itself at other times as well and can be overcome, usually to the detriment of the body. As in the case of childbirth when the baby will probably emerge naturally with the life force but some bright spark wants to say 'push' and not let life force impulses just happen. The same is true for having a poo when people give

9

themselves piles by straining, when all they need to do is to not override the life force urges when they come.

If you have ever been addicted to any drug like nicotine, alcohol or sugar, and tried to give it up, you will have experienced the pull of life force in a distorted way and know it can be very strong. Everyone alive has experienced life force and continues to experience it.

Using the life force in daily life

If you have not consciously thought about the life force before now you might be forgiven for thinking that it doesn't matter whether you connect with it or not. Connecting with it enables you to understand why you have good days and bad days, why you can't do the things you say you want to do like lose weight, exercise regularly, meditate, not get angry, not be compulsive or obsessive. Understanding the life force allows you to become aware of your faults and do something about them. Not everyone wants to but if you do then carry on reading.

It doesn't matter how much you know, there is always more to know. Every few months there are headlines in the media talking about a breakthrough in understanding of some disease or other. And while scientists might make a breakthrough in the understanding of the mechanics of a disease there will never be a chemical cure to any disease without reference to the life force. There might be a chemical relief of a symptom but the disease is made up of more than symptoms. The disease is a distortion in the flow of life force, which chemicals don't directly touch. The only solution to these diseases is to deal with the distortion in the flow of life force and get to the very root of the disease.

Conclusion

There is no objective scientific proof that life force exists or doesn't exist. Some scientists choose to believe we are just a collection of chemicals but those scientists have not managed to create life. Scientists have never created life. There is something they are missing, could it be the unmeasurable life force?

HUMAN BEING

Life force

Ego

I-force

Physical Still point

I-force

Dance

Chapter 2: Human beings and the I-force

I-force - resistance to the life force

Most systems of medicine from around the world use the life force in their diagnoses and interventions. Its flow and power are significant to the health of the patient. When a person has an unimpeded life force they are healthy. Sometimes people can project their own life force and when they do other people can feel it from a distance. Those people light up the room. When it is impeded and restricted you can feel its absence also. Those people are generally ill and can drain your energy and even the atmosphere in the room. If you learn to tune into this feeling of life force, you can know when and where your life force encounters restrictions and barriers. This is crucial to an understanding of health.

There is a part in everyone that when they are told they can't do something they say 'Oh yes I can'. That is human nature. This contrary part exists in every age of a person. It exists in a child who is told they can't have sweets in the supermarket and has a tantrum or steals them, or a slightly older child who is told to go to bed and refuses, or a teenager who skips a day of school, or a student who refuses to take an exam, or a worker who refuses to follow their manager's instructions, or a worker who stands up for their rights, or a golfer who smashes their club in frustration or a pensioner who refuses to take their medicine. Animals do this as well but human beings seem to have made an art out of it.

I call this contrary energy the I-force. Pioneers of all kinds have this energy, they do something they are told can't be done or they see something that they don't like and want it changed. Life force is in there but also the stubborn energy that opposes it and using those two forces in tandem is what gives that person the power to do what they do. Together these two forces are the energy behind everything that has ever been created by a human being. From the ceiling in the Sistine Chapel to the Clifton Suspension Bridge, from early cave art to present-day graffiti, all have been created by a combination of the life force and I-force.

These two forces together have created buildings, books, music, films, art, science but also disputes, war, illness and depression. That's a pretty powerful couple of forces. Within us, the life force and the I-force interact with each other and outwardly react with the world. They become our personalities. And when the I-force gets a little too strong and overcomes the life force, and stays fixed, we get told by our body in the form of symptoms. Our ego and personality are made up of a combination of I-forces.

Life force and I-force together are also the energy behind us doing things that we know are harmful to us, like smoking, drinking, overeating and even having affairs. It's not that those activities are inherently bad; it's that they exist because of our I-force.

As the I-force gets stronger and more dominant, it creates more health issues for us. Our mind/body knows that a strong, fixed I-force is a problem and sends us messages in the form of symptoms to tell us. Our response, Western medicine's response, is generally to remove the body's ability to produce that symptom through medication. Stopping the message allows us to continue with the behaviour that created the symptom which in turn necessitates more medicine.

This I-force power comes from its ability to resist the life force. In the same way that the power of a river may be small but when there is resistance to its flow created by a dam, the energy that builds up behind the dam can be massive. Without the life force, there would be no I-force.

Each fixed part of the I-force will eventually create a symptom. The symptom is the mind/body's attempt to show its owner where there is a problem. The symptom is not the problem, it is the messenger. If the problem is resolved the symptoms go away.

The life force is infinite, at least I have never reached the end of it, just like the river keeps flowing. The I-force, on the other hand, is finite - created in part by our experiences and is like the finite dam.

'If the doors of perception were cleansed every thing would appear to man as it is, infinite. For man has closed himself up, till he sees all things thro' narrow chinks of his cavern." William Blake (From The Marriage of Heaven and Hell)

So, the life force in conjunction with the I-force has created everything man-made on this planet, including illnesses and diseases.

Feeling the life force in another person

People instinctively know that touch is an intimate form of connection, one that can reach their essence. This is why you only allow certain people to touch you. When you touch someone who is re-experiencing a trauma you are saying 'I am here' and it is possible for them to 'hear' you - but touch is the way you are communicating, not language.

When you see your child involved in a potentially

traumatic incident the impulse is to hold them. What you are doing is connecting your two life forces. When two life forces connect they join and the less experienced person can feel comforted from the more experienced. Parents know this, people know this, instinctively.

The case of the moving shoulder

Trauma isn't just a psychological phenomenon. I remember in 1995 when for the first time I put my hand on a person's traumatised shoulder. The person concerned had been in a road traffic accident a few years before and he told me the pain had come from the seat belt during the collision. Of course, there was a bit more to it than that, in that the injuries incurred by other people involved in the accident were serious. Anyway, when I connected to his life force at his shoulder movements started occurring. In retrospect, I realised the movements were exactly the movements his shoulder went through at the time of the accident. We were both sufficiently interested to see where it all went and the movements continued and became painful. I asked if he could cope with the pain and he said he could, so we continued.

The movements continued. I felt like I could feel the whole accident slowly unfolding and resolving. It was more than just physical movements I could feel - there were locked-in emotional issues, from the trauma, that I could feel surfacing too. How do I know that I wasn't making it up? Ultimately, there is no objective proof, but I know myself. I know that the feelings I was going through weren't mine. I didn't have experience of the accident and they were not emotional problems, they were distortions in the flow of life force that showed up in the patient as unresolved emotional activity. In my case, I was more aware of them as just distortions in the flow of life force. I knew the feelings I experienced did not belong to me but belonged to the patient. This made them easier to bear and I could follow them to a still point and not try to escape from them. In doing this his shoulder healed.

Practising the Boulderstone Technique

Whenever you get close to another human being there is a charge. If you get too close by 'invading their space' that charge increases. Most people can feel when someone gets too close to them. When I practise the Boulderstone Technique I hold someone's head in my hands and am open to what they feel. Provided I have dropped feelings of power or fear, I can feel, or sense, their life force. That's what I feel. It goes beyond plain physical touch. At this level it isn't sexual in any way, there is no power issue, it is a connection that is profound and real and relaxed. There is no judgement because if I do start judging I lose my 'stillness' and the connection. When I connect completely with another human being my awareness of the whole world drops away, time disappears and thinking slows. It is possible to have this connection with a 'patient', a pet, a child, a lover or anyone but it only happens if you don't judge and your mind is 'still'.

Once connected, the world of the 'patient' opens up. This isn't mind reading but something I can feel. If there is no problem the life force remains 'clear', capable of moving in any direction without restriction and there isn't anything to feel, no restricted flow of life force, no I-force. However, that isn't how patients come to me. Patients come to me when they need help, so this isn't what I generally feel. When people come to see me they tend to have compartmentalised their problems. People hide away their traumas and things that stress them so they can get on with their day but if they bring an issue to the fore, when I'm connected to them in the way just described, that difficulty, their problem, is felt as a tension. Although the connected feeling is physical there is also an emotional component to it that comes in the form of empathy. It's difficult to describe because it's something that is felt or sensed. What I say about what I feel is that I can feel the distortion in the flow of life force around their problems when I connect with them. In moments of difficulty, ie. when they are focussed on something unresolved, the life force flow changes from being 'clear' and relaxed to being 'distorted'. (More in Chapter 3.)

Do it now, not tomorrow

If you dealt with your problems as they arose you would have no restrictions in the flow of life force. But dealing with problems as they arise isn't always possible. Sometimes problems appear too big and you need to deal with them slowly, at a later date, in a safer place or in smaller pieces. When this happens you can distort the flow of life force so that you can avoid dealing with the problem head-on. That might seem clever but if you don't deal with the problem the distortion in the flow of life force remains and symptoms of some kind always result. The symptoms are there to tell you there is still a distortion that needs to be sorted. Generally, most people think that once their problem has been 'put away' that is the end of it. Problems that have been 'put away' but are not properly dealt with will always eventually lead to symptoms and pain. Not dealing with problems is a major cause of our diseases and illnesses.

The case of Laura

Laura couldn't get to peace and the still point. Somehow she had confused the still point with dying and quite sensibly wanted to avoid it. The problem with this situation was that her problems were building up. Rather than clearing anything she put them in a mental bucket and hid them away. As time went by she had to become sharper and sharper, using her I-force to keep any reminders of her problems at bay. Her I-force had a big job to do and the size of the job was increasing every time she didn't deal with a problem. She knew when something was going to remind her of an unresolved issue and smartly brought up her I-force. She was verbally and emotionally quick. She had a few issues like claustrophobia (her bucket was filling up) and headaches (it was all a mess). But when menopause turned up her world was thrown upside down and she lost the ability to recognise when an issue was about to surface. Her secure world fell apart, her anxiety increased, she became jittery and had difficulty sleeping. She was put on hormone replacement therapy by her doctor which initially helped (but didn't solve the problem). With my help, I taught Laura to move to a still point and relax the use of the I-force. Once she got the idea, she could do it for herself. She learnt how she previously had used the I-force to avoid problems and now could get to a still point. She fully recovered and got control back in her life.

Our body always knows the cause

Every illness has a cause and that cause is a distortion in the flow of life force. I am not talking about bacteria and viruses. Bacteria or viruses might be present but there is always something that happens before the bugs come along. (More on this in Chapter 5.)

If you have a problem that produces symptoms, that you weren't born with, then there was a time when the problem wasn't there. That problem has a cause because there isn't anything in the world that happens for no reason, and that includes illnesses. Most illnesses are self-limiting and disappear on their own without medication if left alone and there are no underlying problems. Headaches, a cold, influenza, diarrhoea and others usually fall into this category. Some illnesses may become chronic (lasting more than six months) but even so, there is still a cause. The problem didn't just arise out of nowhere. What I am saying might seem obvious but I have heard it reported many times by patients that their doctors told them that they are just 'unlucky' with their diagnosis, that 'It could have happened to anyone'. That is not the case; you might not know how it occurred but every illness that has ever occurred has happened for a reason. and that reason always comes down to a distortion in the flow of life force.

It is empowering to understand that all symptoms and diseases are there as a reaction to a distortion in the flow of life force. Knowing this means you can do something about it, even before there are symptoms. All serious illnesses, including cancer, start out as a small distortion and only grow if ignored or suppressed. These small distortions may be felt by the patient or a practitioner.

When I'm treating a patient, if they connect with any problem of theirs, I can feel the generated distortion in the flow of life force. This can be felt before the patient even voices the problem. It doesn't matter if that problem is physical, mental, emotional or spiritual, it can be felt. If it is the cause of their illness we can go into it and resolve it. I can ask the patient questions around the problem and they don't even need to answer. I can feel their response, often one that exists before thinking kicks in and we can work with that.

When the life force runs 'clear' the person is at peace, in a still point. Whenever they connect with an inner contradiction they move from 'clear' to 'restricted', from still point to being in the dance, and that is palpable.

And so what I am feeling when I am connected to another person, and feel a distortion in the flow of life force, is the cause of their symptoms. Human beings have this special gift of putting off dealing with problems but the price is pain and restriction, either physical, mental/ emotional or spiritual. It is the ego, powered by the I-force, that causes this pain and restriction.

If a problem hasn't been fully processed, whenever the person gets close to that problem and it is triggered (through seeing a film, reading a book or perhaps hearing a story that somehow reflects their own problem) a backing away or restriction occurs. The person involved may cringe, go quiet, change the subject or run away. This is what I am calling distortion in the flow of life force. When doing something they know they shouldn't, they create a distortion. They resist the thing that distorted the flow of life force and they may even try to deny it and say they are fine when they aren't. But their body knows and reacts truthfully, even if their ego doesn't want to, and that feeling is palpable. And because it is palpable it can be treated.

Ego, persona and personality

Who are you? This is the age-old question that seekers from all over the world have sought to answer.

We all have a personality that is made up of different personas. Our different personas are created, by our ego, to help us communicate with different people. We may be a father, or a worker, or a boss, or a brother or a bossy brother and all of these require different personas. The different personas are comprised of the life force and I-force and contain our values, things we are attracted to and repulsed by. The more consistent we are across our personas the happier we will be and the less effort we need to keep it all together. Sometimes these personas will be at odds with one another. For example, you may behave differently towards your children than you might towards your friends. In that difference, there can lie all sorts of conflicts which you have to be easy with and you have to be easy moving between them. If you aren't easy moving between them one will bleed into another causing you to seem hypocritical. For example, if you ignore your brother hurting himself with drinking and smoking but you tell your husband to stop, eventually, friction will arise.

We all have a physical body that feels physical sensations and a personality that has thoughts and emotions. Like everyone, I think some nice things, such as: 'She looks good wearing that', and some nasty things, such as: 'What a hideous dress'. I have nice feelings: love, and nasty feelings: jealousy, and I have physical feelings that are comforting, and physical feelings that are uncomfortable, but the one thing I know about all of these things is that they are unique and together they add up to me. All these thoughts, feelings and physical sensations are created by my human ability to resist the life force. So, in one sense, I can say I am made up of the life force and the resistance to the life force, ie the I-force.

The life force, working together and in opposition to the I-force, pulling and pushing around my thoughts, feelings and physical body, defines 'me', my personality. The personality is dynamic and continually changing. It is unique. There might be a bit more to me in the form of desires and aversions, loves and hates but still, these are fundamentally made up of the life force and I-force in conjunction with my body, feelings and thoughts.

The ego is the part that sees a need for and creates the personas. The personas together make our personality.

There is no problem with any ego while it remains flexible.

How we get ill

The ego creates personas by employing the I-force to temporarily restrict the life force. This can appear useful to the ego for many reasons. An ego likes to get what it wants. A large, fixed ego will get what it wants too often. We all know the larger-than-life characters who have large egos but there is a downside to having a large, fixed ego. When this ego starts to believe it is more important than everyone else and doesn't know how to be humble, problems will arise. The ego can stay humble and be flexible by accessing a still point. When the ego first becomes fixed the restriction to the life force may appear strong but later, through lack of flexibility, it will become brittle and crumble. This happens to everything that has a life force and doesn't access its still point, from the Roman Empire to any dictator you can mention.

Our greatest enemy is not what's out there; it's what's in here. - S.D. Gupta

In the individual, a strong ego will be helpful at the beginning but later, without flexibility, it will cause conflicts and produce symptoms. The symptoms are to show the ego where it needs to change.

These symptoms can be anything from cancer to anger, compulsions, superstitions or even depression, self-harm and phobias. And they are only there because they are trying to show you where the problem is. Cover over the symptoms and they get worse in order to show you the way.

The purpose of the ego is to get something done but at its core is a still point and emptiness. The ego doesn't want to know this. The ego equates emptiness with nothingness and death but the ego doesn't want this to be true. If it was true then that would mean its life is pointless. And so it tries to cover this emptiness by making noise and distracting its owner with a dance. What it doesn't know is that emptiness and nothingness are different (see chapter 6).

The ego fears death. If you say you don't fear death you are either lying or understand that ultimately the ego is unimportant. Sometimes a person who believes the ego is everything becomes aware that there is only emptiness at its core and then wonders what the point in anything is and falls into depression, has a mid-life crisis or even commits suicide. You can sometimes see this happening to celebrities who need a big ego to do their 'job' but know they have no substance and self-medicate with alcohol or other drugs to distract them from this tricky dilemma.

Another solution, that some celebrities have found, is to remain humble and realise that the ego is essentially selfish and only looks out for itself. Countering the ego with humbleness, the opposite of what it wants, can work if they have friends and family they trust. You hear those celebrities say 'my family and friends keep my feet on the ground'. Yet another solution is to 'find God'. Counteracting the ego belief that it is a god with a 'real' God, outside of you, can be a solution for some.

Having success in life often develops a big ego which can be difficult to maintain and not always worth the effort. Meditation, or dealing with the things that come up when it approaches emptiness, is another solution to an overdeveloped ego (see Chapter 9).

Becoming a person with a fixed ego means that you will eventually get ill. You have to, that is a consequence of creating an ego by distorting the flow of life force. However, when you can find the still point within yourself, which means letting go of your fixed ego, you will be healthy again. Most of us need some help with this.

The story and the dance are constructions of the ego

Whenever people come to see me with a problem they usually want to talk about what has happened to them. But what they say has happened to them is never the whole truth even though they rarely lie. When we see the complete truth, from every angle, all problems go away. I have seen this time and time again. It doesn't matter what has happened to a person, it is *always* possible to live in peace. But the dance (meaning the illusions of the ego) is still the dance and, for some, the dance seems more attractive than a still point. People hold on to their story as if it is reality but it is always a refection of reality.

Something I would like to tell everyone is that the dance is temporary but the still point is forever. In other words, many people know they have to address something within their story but put it off. If they dealt with that issue the problem would go away. Usually, it feels like addressing the issue is harder than putting up with the symptom and so they don't address the issue. Domestic abuse can fall into this category. Is it easier to put up with abuse for ten minutes once a week than spend a month or two in gut wrenching fear? The answer, of course, is that those ten minutes mount up over the years to be much longer than a couple of months.

Instead, people suffer, headaches perhaps. But they know if they addressed the cause of the headache, while it might appear to be more difficult than having the headache, they would only have to do it once. Not addressing the cause could give monthly headaches for years. Still, they choose regular headaches over a perceived more difficult resolution.

The *story* that has brought anyone to the point of illness isn't the problem. Getting justice changes little. Being heard changes little. As has been said by many people, 'There's your truth, there's my truth and there's what happened', meaning we all see things from our ego's perspective and it isn't complete. When we see something with no ego involvement there is no judgment and no blame. From a healing perspective the dance isn't the whole story because it doesn't help solve the issues that arise. From a human point of view the dance or story about what has happened might be interesting to hear but relating it completely can take a long time, is often very difficult and, even when heard by another person, doesn't solve much. This is partly due to the inadequacy of language to correctly describe the distortion.

The story is what counsellors often want you to relate and they believe this is the route to healing. But the real problem is the distortion in the flow of life force and the inability to reach the still point. Relating the story is really dancing around the problem because the story is a translation into words of this distortion. Unpacking the story to clear the problem can take years and is incredibly inefficient.

The story and the dance, however, do give access to where the distortion is, and therefore it gives access to the real problem. For example, the story might be that somebody was involved in a road traffic accident that involved fatalities and where they had hit their head and weeks afterwards realised their memory wasn't functioning as it was before. The problem may well be physical (where they hit their head), but it is more likely that the people that died in the road traffic accident have had more of an impact on the person than they realised, and in trying to forget the whole incident their mind is obligingly allowing them to forget everything else as well.

When I work on the distortion in the flow of life force, as opposed to the story, the problems clear in the most efficient way possible, in exactly the right order, because it is the order the patient has created them in, and I don't need to hear the story because I follow the flow of life force. (More on how in Chapter 3.) Not having to relate their story in great depth can be liberating to any patient - I merely require them to think about the worst aspect of their story and that is enough to give me access to the whole distortion and also the solution and still point.

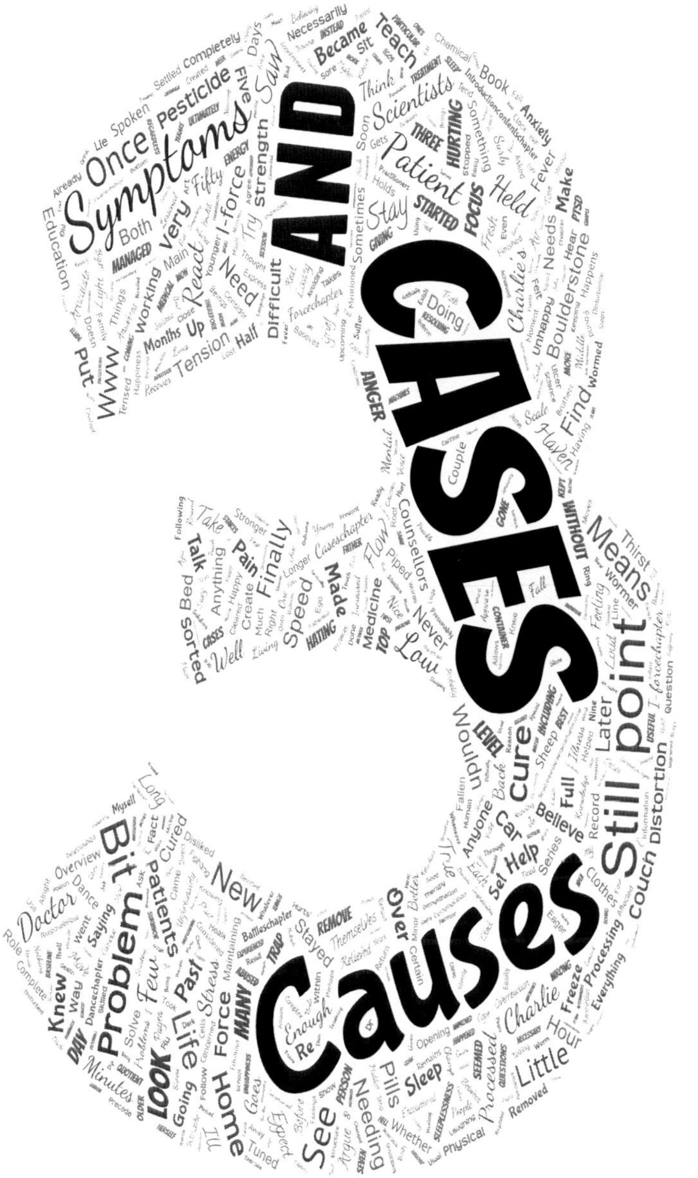
Causes
AND
CASES

Chapter 3: Causes and Cases

The case of Charlie

I saw Charlie for the first time when he was 16. He came in with his mother, and my first impression was that he seemed a nice person if a bit surly. My opening question to most patients is 'On a scale of 0 to 100, how happy are you?' After a little bit of contemplation, Charlie answered 62. This I considered low but his mother piped up that he was in the middle of exams and we should expect it to be low.

Charlie's main problem, as far as his mother was concerned, was that he was always getting into fights with his younger sister and, being older and stronger, he was hurting her.

So I got Charlie on the couch, held his head, tuned into his life force, and asked out loud a series of questions that might help point me (and him) to his problem or problems. In Charlie's case it soon became clear he only had one problem. As I asked about school, his tension increased and when I asked about exams, in particular, he tensed up even more. I couldn't do anything about him having exams, but I could do something about Charlie's reaction to them. And so I set about removing the tension that came up when he thought about his upcoming exams. This felt to me like PTSD, something I have encountered with many patients, and after working with it for about five minutes, I felt there was no stress left. He went home and he stopped getting into fights with his sister.

Was this a good outcome? How can we tell? His mother was happy with the outcome, and presumably, his sister was as well. Charlie was relieved his stress had lessened. It was a good outcome all round, as far as it went.

However, if you believe this was a good outcome, you

have fallen into the same trap that Western medical practitioners fall into after giving a medicine that appears to 'work' and that is believing that removing the symptom is the same as removing the problem. It isn't. What we haven't done is go back to the baseline and asked how happy he is now. If he says 95 or higher I have probably helped as much as I can at the moment. However, he told me his happiness quotient had gone up from 62 to 75. There was more to do, but he didn't know what else was wrong. So, I was left with a situation where the patient couldn't articulate what his problem was.

Talking about problems is only useful to certain people. But because I am feeling a distortion in the flow of life force, talking about the problem isn't always necessary. I already had enough information to work with. Charlie said he was only 75% happy and so that unhappiness was my new starting point.

At the next appointment things with his sister had settled down and he wasn't getting into fights. And so, on the couch, I asked Charlie to focus on the 'only feeling 75% happy'. And he did. I could feel the restriction and knew something wasn't right. There was an I-force block, which I got Charlie to focus on. We stayed with the problem until the life force started to move through it and clear it. The I-force block started resolving and over the next few minutes, Charlie completely cleared it. My role was to keep him focussed while the life force did its job. When there was no life force disturbance left Charlie went home. I didn't hear from him for a while.

I later found out that Charlie had finished his exams and had left school. At this point, he was finally able to articulate that he didn't like school, that it had made him very unhappy. In fact, he had always disliked it but because he thought it was compulsory and he therefore didn't have a choice about going, he had never mentioned it.

So what do I really do? I teach people to find the still point within themselves and when they can't find it because it is disturbed by the I-force, I look for the block that is in the way, I teach people to stay focussed and follow the life force to stillness.

You could argue that to get an education you have to stay at school even if it means that you're going to be unhappy - this is a situation many young people find themselves in. I would argue that being happy is the best education anyone could have. That doesn't mean running away to do something frivolous and avoiding responsibilities. That isn't happiness. Happiness means you can sit in a still point knowing there is no inner voice saying "I should have done this" or "I could have done that".

Happiness doesn't mean you are continually laughing; it means that you know everything is alright, and nothing is out of place, meaning the I-force isn't fighting your life force. But fighting isn't necessarily a problem. You might be a professional boxer fighting in the ring. If you can remain in a still point then fighting is what you should be doing. Regardless of whether you are fighting or not, happiness is when you are in a still point.

The case of Jo

Between the ages of seven and nine Jo was sexually abused by her father. After more than fifty years it still affected her. It made relationships difficult. Her brothers and sisters wouldn't agree on whether it happened or if it happened then perhaps she should consider herself lucky! It was all messed up. Messed up then and messed up now. But why is it messed up now, fifty years later? What holds the problem in place? Can it ever be sorted out or must the survivor continue to suffer for as long as she lives?

The story isn't the problem

For way too long Western medical counsellors have focussed on the story of the problem. The story is what happened to the patient. The patient may be reluctant to talk about it because it brings up difficult emotions or they may be eager to talk about it but, either way, the solution doesn't lie in keeping the story hidden or relating the story, however much counsellors think it does. The problem doesn't need to be told, instead it needs to be *processed*. It is true that sometimes this can be achieved by just talking about it. But this way is inefficient since words can only express what has happened when they are spoken by skilled people. It is time-consuming because talking about it can take months or years and sometimes it can even be re-traumatising.

I believe the real problem, and the reason the problem is kept in place, is the **ego's fear of the overwhelm.** As a result an I-force structure is created that protects the ego from this overwhelm. The ego's fear of overwhelm is what needs to be addressed. The truth is we can all cope with whatever is thrown at us, that is the bottom line. But if we are inexperienced in processing complex and/or traumatic problems, there is a tendency to freeze, to jam things up, so that nothing moves. We keep the problem in place through our I-force. We get stuck.

The ego believes it can stop itself suffering by using the I-force to freeze the processing. It is true that if the ego freezes everything it won't feel the difficulty but, unfortunately, this also stops the processing of the problem. In other words by resisting the feelings of the problem, the problem gets held in place and it remains unresolved. So, what is to be done?

If I can monitor the amount of overwhelm experienced by the patient and know how to slow it down whenever it starts to get too much, I can direct the patient to work through the trauma in a comfortable way. If I can couple this with maintaining a still point, it can keep the patient on track with an overview. It is then possible to clear problems completely at the speed of the patient's thoughts. I can do this because I can feel both the life force and I-force of the patient.

Jo complete

Jo needed one session to undo the trauma of her past, including coming to terms with how her family treated her. They didn't need to be present, she did it on her own. Jo came back to see me twice more to check that things were sorted and to clear up some minor things that came to light after the major trauma was processed. We are still in touch but I don't expect that aspect of her past to cause her any more troubles. It is resolved and she has found a still point. Once you have found the still point in a trauma you can return to it more easily.

It is the close contact of connecting with a patient's life force and I-force and maintaining a still point that is the difference with my therapy. This knowledge allows the speed with which a patient can clear themselves to be regulated by the patient's speed of thought. I don't make suggestions as to how the patient has to behave or think or tell them to 'go to their special place'. All of that will get done automatically by the patient, silently and intuitively. I don't have to ask the patient to tell me their story. Very few words need to be spoken. Healing takes place on a life force/I-force level. It is beyond language.

Any symptom can have any cause

A patient may go to a Western medical doctor saying 'my head hurts' and get pain killers, or they might say 'I can't sleep' and get sleeping pills, or 'I have a fever' and get antibiotics, or say 'I'm anxious' or 'I can't stop crying' and get anti-depressants. The doctor's pills may make the symptoms go away, but that doesn't necessarily mean the patient is cured, or even that their health has improved.

The hurting head could be the result of the fear of losing a job or grief. The sleeplessness could be the result of grief or hating life as it is. The fever could be the result of hating life or anger. The anxiety could be the result of anger and fear of losing a job. Any symptom can have any 'cause'. But while the symptom may point to the cause, it isn't the cause itself.

Mental and emotional problems often precede physical symptoms but that doesn't mean they are the primary cause of the illness. They also have a cause.

Remove the real cause and the problem goes away

I have found that once the real cause of any illness (including anxiety, depression, migraines, sleeplessness, fever or even a swollen knee or an ulcer) has been removed, then the illness also goes away. When all egos are out of the way, the body and mind heals itself.

Illness, both physical and mental, is described by its symptoms but is only cured by dealing with its root cause and that cause is the distortion in the flow of life force. In the following pages I will try to show how this very simple cause exists for all illnesses and once that is removed it leads to a resolution of symptoms and cure of the illness itself.

'There is but one cure in disease; the body's ability to heal itself. And there is only one thing that any doctor can do for a patient. And that is to remove an obstruction to healing thus facilitating it.'
Dr Fred Barge

There is no doubt that science took the healing art out of a dark place. Medical science has its place but human beings react differently to the same stimulus. If we did all react in the same way, like machines, then medical science would have been able to eradicate all our symptoms without introducing new ones. Medical scientists tend to look at things on a microscopic level rather than taking an overview. Medical scientists don't fully understand what elements are needed to create a living being. If they did they would have been able to artificially create life and that hasn't happened. There is more to human beings than science has so far discovered. Human beings, and all living things, have something in them that has so far managed to elude science. That something may be the life force.

Medical scientists are given problems to solve, and they solve them but, while they don't use the life force, they don't have the complete picture. For example, it is relatively easy to say that Multiple Sclerosis is caused by demyelination of nerve cells because that is what mechanically happens. So, a medical scientist will look for a way to stop the demyelination. What they haven't understood is that the demyelination has a cause that is connected to the I-force. Without this knowledge, all 'cures' that stop demyelination will only be half the story and ultimately fail. (More on MS in Chapter 7)

The story about how you got here isn't important (unless the story continues)

The idea that the patient has caused their own symptoms doesn't sit well with patients. Why would they want to make their life worse after experiencing an overwhelming episode that created their symptoms? If they created their symptoms why can't they undo them? In fact, even doctors don't want patients to accept they are responsible for their health. Doctors go out of their way to assume responsibility for the health of their patients so that the patient can believe they are not responsible for their illness. This situation has occurred because both doctors and patients believe that the symptoms are the bad guys and need to be eliminated.

Panic attacks (see Trauma, PTSD and Panic Attacks) are a good example of why and how a patient may create their symptoms. A common complaint amongst people who have panic attacks is that they can come from out of the blue. They can occur even when the patient is in a relaxed mood and safe environment. They can seem pointless. But the relaxed mood and safe environment are exactly the point. If you know you are safe, what can harm you? You can process the memory knowing nothing can harm you. You can get to the other side, maintaining a still point so that the next time the panic attack happens you can cope with it. It is very clever of the mind to realise this. But generally people don't understand. In the same way some people believe what is happening on the television screen is real, people having a panic attack (memory replayed) can believe they are actually reliving something dreadful rather than having a memory of it. They have forgotten that they are currently safe. And the replaying of the trauma is an attempt to get the patient to look at the whole episode *while connected to a still point and thus clear it*. The next time the replay occurs it will be easier to work through. And even more so the next time. Each time it is worked through it gets easier.

The place where the symptoms come from is the problem, not the symptoms. Believing the symptoms are more important than the cause is like the turning off the smoke alarm instead of putting out the fire.

Case: Chris Mepham (in his own words)

I was working as a sheep farmer, in June 1998, and it was time to worm the sheep. I put the plastic container on my back, full of the usual pesticide. I had to squirt a measure of it into each sheep's mouth. Unfortunately, unknown to me, the container was leaking for about an hour and a half before I realised that it had soaked through all my clothes and onto my back and down my legs. I changed my clothes, washed the chemical off myself, and carried on with my work.

I became seriously unwell. I had a metallic taste on my tongue, a sore throat and a tremendous thirst. I needed to drink three or four pints of water every hour around the clock, as nothing would slake my thirst. I could only breathe about 80%. It felt like my lungs just wouldn't inflate. My thighs, calves and biceps hurt like hell and my muscles just wouldn't work. Nothing could relieve the pain, not moving or staying still. I had no energy to talk and couldn't feed myself or go to the bathroom. One of the worst things was I couldn't sleep although I was desperately tired so there was no respite. I stayed awake all day and all night. I had a headache and a bad cough and assumed I must have a serious bout of flu. I was off work for three days, then gradually recovered over 2 or 3 months, until I wormed the sheep again.

Again, I went down with a bang, this time needing a full week in bed, with the same symptoms as before, and needing even longer to recover. I still didn't connect the illness with the sheep wormer. This reaction happened every time I wormed the sheep, needing to take more time off in bed and longer to recover each time. Each time I lost a full stone in weight, which I managed to put back on afterwards. This continued for 4 years.

Finally, in 2002, I went to a London hospital to see if they thought it could be the sheep wormer making me ill and to see if anyone could help. Off the record, they told me it almost certainly was the pesticide, but they couldn't acknowledge this on record as they received so much funding from the drug company that made the pesticide!

All they could suggest was that I stay away from all chemicals and get plenty of fresh air, exercise and a good diet.

Well, fresh air didn't cure the problem. When the same symptoms occurred again, I was more ill than ever. I was sceptical about trying alternative medicine, but desperate enough to try anything, as by now I felt I was at death's door. When I first turned up at The Boulderstone Technique clinic I was so dazed I hardly knew where I was. I was so weak I couldn't get out of the car and walk, so the practitioner had to treat me in the car.

After this first treatment, I felt somewhat better. I finally managed to sleep for a couple of hours which felt like a miracle. It was the first time I had been able to sleep in 6 or 7 days. I came back the following day. The second treatment was like turning a light switch on. My energy came flooding back and I felt so much better.

I went from strength to strength until I got my old strength back.

(End of Chris's statement.)

What had happened was that Chris's body had detected

that it was being poisoned with sheep dip. In this situation, its first job was to ensure Chris's survival. It struggled but ultimately it found a way. However, the reaction was extreme, it needed to be, and every time the body thought it saw the problem happening again it went into defence mode and overreacted. We all do it. If something life-threatening happens to us we remember the situation and know how to react. But the detection of chemical bug killer wasn't the problem. The problem was the overreaction, the I-force doing a little too much. It discovers a poison in the air and screams 'ARRGH'.

The overreaction, by the I-force, comes about because something isn't processed and leaves a shadow that can get re-stimulated by similar triggers. In the next chapter, this idea is used in the definition of health.

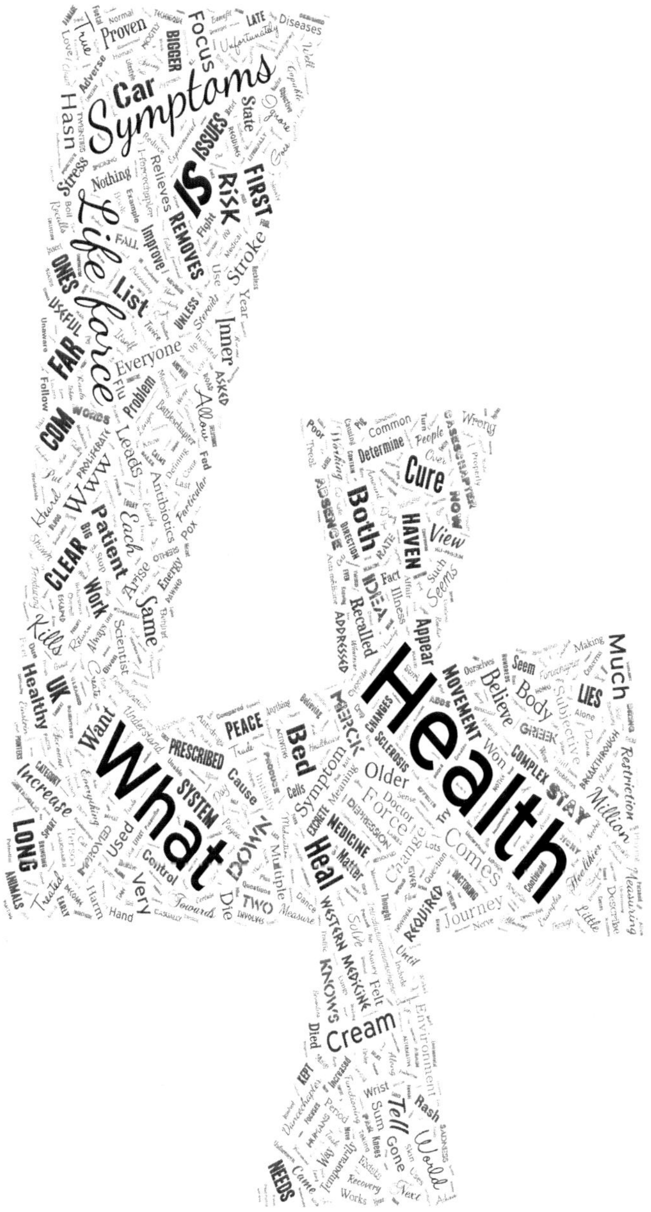

Chapter 4: What is health?

As you get older your health concerns change. At the start of your life you don't even think about your health, unless you have a big problem. I was probably fed up that I was kept in bed while I had measles or flu or chicken pox and it only slowly dawned on me, when I got into my late twenties, that I could affect my health by my behaviours. I was so unaware it was laughable. Nowadays, I realise I escaped those early years with only a few problems. It could have been a lot worse. Those problems, with my knees, feet, lungs, back, wrist and hand, all continue to affect me in my seventies and come from playing sport, smoking and other reckless activities. But are they symptoms? What is health? What is illness and what is disease?

Western medicines are designed to deal with symptoms, not health

To determine the health of a person, from a Western medical point of view, is a complex affair. It involves taking scans, looking at blood work, investigating history and current lifestyle, questions about relationships, phobias and compulsions. The list could go on and on. Instead, Western medical doctors only casually ask about your health. What they mostly want to know about is your current symptoms.

By having the focus of attention on symptoms, rather than health, it is possible to forget what you are trying to achieve. Scientists can find drugs that make it impossible for symptoms to even appear. This only seems like a good idea because the illness is understood as a collection of symptoms. If the illness is seen as a distortion in the flow of life force and the symptoms as pointers to where that distortion is, then removing the symptoms is like removing the warning lights in a car. Just because the lights don't come on any more doesn't mean the car is in good health.

Everyone knows this, including doctors, but they still prescribe medicines that they know don't improve the health of people even if they remove symptoms. And they don't always remove symptoms. Medicines don't always work.

There have been literally hundreds of drug withdrawals worldwide in recent years. These were drugs that the pharmaceutical companies that made them said were 'safe and effective'. They were tested by scientists and drug trials and were supposedly proven to be 'safe and effective'. They weren't; they had side effects and caused unforeseen problems. Side effects included foetal abnormalities, severe depression, psychosis, carcinomas, heart, liver and kidney damage, stroke and death. These aren't insignificant side effects. If Western medicine uses tried and tested science, how has this happened? Each of the withdrawn medicines must have been proven, by science, to be capable of doing its job and be safe but something went wrong. My view of it is that current scientific understanding isn't enough to determine what is 'safe and effective'.

The symptoms alone aren't the illness. Instead, they are the body's best way of expressing the real problem. Take the symptoms away without dealing with the problem and the body will have to come up with the next best way of expressing the problem. The next best way of expressing the problem will always contain symptoms that are worse than the original ones.

For example, Multiple Sclerosis (MS) is an illness that is misunderstood. Most doctors and scientists see MS as a demyelination of nerve cells that leads to pain and badly functioning nerves. Demyelination certainly occurs but doctors tell my patients that they do not know the cause. I have treated many people who have been diagnosed with MS and all of them have emotional issues that they have been unable to resolve. On top of this, they often have a relapse because of a stressful situation that either adds to or compounds their problem. Very often they self-prescribe cannabis. It temporarily calms the stress and relieves symptoms but does absolutely nothing for the real problem. The real problem is not knowing how to deal with stress and emotional issues. What can a body do? When the effects of the cannabis wear off, it will try again with more symptoms and, if it has enough energy, turn up the intensity of the symptoms so it can be heard. Cannabis relieves the symptoms and it is probably on a par with the Western medical approach of steroids but neither deal with the real problem, only the symptoms. (More on MS in Chapter 7)

Sometimes, treating symptoms is exactly what is needed, especially if there is a life-threatening incident that needs to be resolved. When you have been in a road traffic accident you need your physical symptoms addressed before you ask about the causes of the problem. However, sometimes resolving the symptoms isn't enough.

I don't think the problem lies with science but there is something wrong with the way science is employed by Western medical scientists. In order to state that a particular medicine is safe and effective, it would make sense if the health of the person taking it could be measured before and after taking any experimental drug, so any health changes could be monitored and compared. Given an experimental drug, a patient's symptoms might completely disappear and if there are no related new symptoms it could be classified as safe and effective. New, unrelated symptoms could arise, ones that weren't being measured but if the overall health of the patient isn't being measured you wouldn't know. A declaration of 'safe and effective' to a new drug where the health of the guinea pig is not measured is false. Yet that is what is done.

Western medical scientists understand the mechanics of many diseases; they know how they function. But that isn't enough. We need to know what is going on in the health of the individual and for that you need an understanding of the life force. The World Health Organisation states, 'There is little evidence that older people today are in better health than their parents.' In other words, Western medicine hasn't improved the health of people in the last twenty-five years or so!

Now we see a possible reason for our health not improving: Western medicine focuses on symptoms because it can't or won't measure the health of a person. Why?

Scientists aren't always medical people. This is sometimes significant if they are asked to solve a problem. For example, medical people might notice that in an infection certain bugs seem to proliferate and if you could find a medicine to kill off those bugs, it would be useful. The task is passed to the scientists and indeed they find a medicine that kills off the bugs and doesn't kill the person. If the person taking the medicine develops paranoid delusions, for example, that would probably not even be noticed by the scientist. The brief was find a medicine that kills off the bugs and doesn't kill the person. The job was done.

Solutions that don't take into account the overall health of the person are likely to create situations that are worse than the original problems. This situation is true in lots of different arenas where there is life force. For example, DDT was developed as a breakthrough insecticide in the 1940s. It was initially used with great effect to kill off malaria, typhus, and other insect-borne human diseases. It also was effective for insect control in crop and livestock production, institutions, homes, and gardens. DDT worked in that it did the job it was asked to do, it killed off the bugs.

Unfortunately, just as the overall health of the patient isn't considered, the overall health of the environment wasn't taken into account.

Thirty years after DDT was introduced it was withdrawn due to its adverse environmental effects on wildlife, as well as its potential human health risks. Since then studies have shown DDT exposure causes adverse effects in humans and is generally considered a carcinogen. A case of the scientist doing their job but not measuring the overall health of the 'patient'.

When any 'breakthrough' is made there are always consequences for the whole community which are often initially ignored. These can be positive and negative. Examples are antibiotics, nuclear weapons, the development of plastics, and genetic modifications to humans, plants and animals.

A person, environment or any entity with a life force isn't the sum of its parts. It is the sum of its parts plus its life force. When it is considered to be the sum of its parts all sorts of problems arise, as can be seen by the DDT example or the pharmaceutical companies producing drugs that deal with some of the parts but later have to be withdrawn. The solution is to look at the life force of the person or environment involved. When you deny the existence of the life force, symptoms become the most important aspect of health. This allows all the symptoms to be treated well but the 'patient' can still be worse off and even die.

Western medicines's obsession with symptoms is seen in the naming of illness

Western medicine locates a symptom and labels it a disease. Examples of this are all those Greek names for illnesses that may describe what is going on but don't look at the cause of the problem. Asthma means 'difficulty breathing', making the symptom the name of the disease. Eczema comes from a Greek word meaning 'to boil' which is meant to describe the skin symptom. Pneumonia means lung condition. Arthritis means disease of the joints - 'itis' meaning inflammation. The disease is named after the symptom.

Some people might say, 'Does it matter, if the symptom/ disease/illness is gone, isn't that health?' Unfortunately, it does matter. If the symptom has been removed by medication but the overall health of the patient hasn't improved, then I believe the patient is probably worse off.

Any one symptom may be caused by different problems. For example, a skin rash could be caused by being sensitive to dairy products or from reacting to a cat. Two different possible causes but only one symptom. In both cases a steroid cream might be prescribed by a Western medical practitioner but the steroid cream would do nothing for either cause and overall, because of side effects of the steroid, would make both patients worse, even if the rash temporarily disappeared.

The cause of the problem (sensitivity to dairy or allergy to cats) hasn't changed so the symptom will return at some point. How many times do patients need a repeat prescription because the cause is never addressed?

Believing that health is only an absence of symptoms belies a misunderstanding of what health is.

Drug recalls

Unfortunately, it is extremely common to hear about a miracle drug that reduces or removes symptoms only for it to be withdrawn later because it creates other serious symptoms or can even result in death. Somehow, the manufacturer 'gets away with it' and can even make money on it.

'Any intelligent fool can make things bigger, more complex and more violent. It takes a touch of genius - and a lot of courage - to move in the opposite direction' - Einstein

---

For example, Vioxx (also known as Rofecoxib) was a painkiller often prescribed to treat pain from arthritis. More than 20 million people (that's a third of the population of the UK) used the drug at its peak, earning approximately $2.5 billion in annual sales for Merck & Co, so potentially as much as $10 billion over the five years it was on the market. (And just to put $10 billion into perspective, because it is an insane amount of money, if you stacked up $1 million in dollar bills it would reach the top of a 30-floor building. That is mad enough but a billion is 1000 times a million! And 10 billion is 10 times that.) Then Merck's own researchers discovered Vioxx increased the chance of heart attack and stroke. One Vioxx report estimated that up to **140,000 people suffered from coronary heart disease** after taking it, with more than 42,000 actually dying. Merck voluntarily recalled Vioxx in 2004. But why are they still in business doing the same thing with other drugs? Is it only about the money? Of course, they had to pay a lot out in compensation but why should they make *any* money out of killing that many people?

This was just one medicine.

Drug recalls are common with over 1,000 a year. The majority (80%) fall in the 'might cause a temporary or slight risk of serious harm' category while 5% fall in the 'is dangerous and poses a serious health risk' category. So if 1000 drugs are recalled a year, 50 of those drugs cause a serious health risk.

The list of recalled medicines is extensive and alarming to see. One of the most damning things the pharmaceutical companies do is withdraw a drug because of injurious side effects in one country but allow it to be sold in another. Putting profits ahead of people's health, and even lives, should result in a criminal offence, in my opinion. Doesn't it make a total mockery of the doctor's oath of 'first do no harm'? The facts are there.

Very rarely does health come from taking drugs. Health doesn't come from stopping the body doing what it wants to do. Health comes from allowing the body to heal itself by *removing the obstacles that are put in its way.*

The difficulties with defining health

Western medicine defines health as a lack of symptoms. If you haven't got any symptoms you are considered healthy, but we know that symptoms can be suppressed. If you need anti-depressants to get out of bed you aren't healthy. All of the anti-drugs fight what the body wants to do. (Antibiotics, anti inflammatories, anti-depressants, antacids, anti-histamines, anti-bacterials, antispasmodics, anti-virals, anti-anxieties). If symptoms are the body's health warning light, taking the anti-medicine is just obscuring the warning. Of course, the body may heal itself in the meantime but by giving the anti-drug you make it a little harder, even if it appears to do good. Defining health as an absence of symptoms is a poor definition of health. Health needs to be defined properly to be able to evaluate whether any medication or medical procedure is useful.

Physical symptoms may seem to have mental or emotional roots

Physical symptoms such as stomach ache, headache, backache or burning sensations can sometimes have a mental or emotional symptom that goes alongside the physical symptom. That does not mean the mental/emotional symptom caused the physical. What happens is the cause, which is a distortion in the flow of life force, causes both. Treating the physical symptoms without looking for the cause isn't going to improve the overall health of the patient in the short or long term.

However, curing most problems of the mind and emotions (like grief, depression, anxiety and overwhelm) is beyond the scope of symptom removal and Western medicine. When you only treat the symptoms and ignore the cause, the original problem always gets worse. How that happens will be explained in Chapter 7.

All symptoms have causes

I have heard many times from my 'Multiple Sclerosis' patients, and others, that their doctors told them their disease came along for 'no reason' or 'out of the blue'. That is absurd. Everything in this life has a cause, including all illnesses. My experience is that every symptom that every person has also has a *palpable* cause. I have yet to come across any symptom that aggravates a patient that I can't feel as a distortion in the flow of life force.

Not uncovering the cause and only treating the symptoms, with doctor-prescribed or even self-prescribed substances, condemns the patient to either a longer recovery time or to having the symptom recur or to driving it deeper and causing it to surface at a later date with more energy (and thus it has escalated to become a bigger problem). Remember, symptoms are the warning lights of the body and just treating the symptoms is like covering up those warning lights. I suppose the hope is that the body will do its magic while the medicine is hiding the problem.

The case of Sarah

A woman aged about 50 came to see me because she was complaining of a few symptoms. After talking to her for a while, I discovered her mother had died prematurely, as far as the patient was concerned, and she had been upset ever since. She told me this quite easily. She had trouble sleeping, anxiety, she didn't want to go out, she couldn't enjoy herself because it would have felt like a betrayal of her mother. She was in grief. She was taking anti-depressants but she said they weren't working because she continued to feel grief.

All of this seems reasonable until I discovered that her mother had died 25 years ago! Now, far be it from me to say that someone should only grieve for a fixed period but I will stick my neck out here and say that 25 years is too long. The major reason this grieving period went on for so long was that the anti-depressants were allowing her to avoid processing her mother's death.

She was currently taking three anti-depressants a day, which had been increased from two a day. I did a quick calculation and discovered that she had possibly swallowed nearly 20,000 anti-depressants and was still no better off. This situation might have continued forever had she not come to see me. Anti-depressants were the doctors only solution, other than referring her to a grief counsellor (which had been done twice and failed twice).

Using the Boulderstone Technique she processed her grief in a single session with two follow up sessions to check because she couldn't believe it. (See Chapter 7: processing an event or trauma).

Western medicine has a poor record when it comes to understanding mental and emotional illnesses. It struggles to define the mind or even agree on whether it exists or not and it also doesn't adequately explain happiness, sadness, pain or love. Having some understanding of the mind, happiness, sadness, love and of course health, is essential if you are to cure emotional and mental illnesses.

The life force and I-force in human beings are not objectively measurable

Feeling the flow of life force in another person can tell you how healthy they are. You can feel how much power they have to resist illness. You can feel how they have distorted the flow of life force. However, it is a subjective and not an objective measurement and it is difficult for scientists to accept the use of subjective measurements.

What's to be done? Ignore the health of the patient but stay objective about symptoms or make subjective judgements about the health of the patient and allow possible human error to creep in?

The point is that human beings aren't machines. There is something about life that scientists haven't nailed down and that is life force.

Anti-medicines

Effort spent researching pharmaceutical drug development may produce financial return but without measuring the effects on health and only measuring the effects on symptoms is only looking at half the story. And while the money may produce a massive profit for a few people it will be at the expense of the health of many others.

And when you look at the anti-drugs (listed above), all of which are working against what the body wants to do, all of them reduce the overall health of the patient. This is a result of the belief that Western medicine knows better than the body. Of course, sometimes that is acceptable. A course of antibiotics which kills off a deadly bacterial infection might also reduce the gut health of a patient for years, but if it keeps the patient alive so that they can build up their health later, isn't that a success? In that case it might be a fair trade. But if the health of the patient isn't measured, where is the science behind that trade off, and how do we weigh up the choice?

Fighting what the body wants to do has to be done in the clear knowledge of why the body is trying to do it in the first place. If you ignore the reasons why the body is doing something and just see a symptom as an unwanted affliction to be removed, you won't be practising healthcare. For example, the temperature of a person often rises when they have an infection. The reason for the rise is that the metabolic rate doubles with each degree increase and a faster metabolic rate will clear the infection quicker. In other words, the body is dealing with the infection more efficiently by causing an increase in temperature.

The knee jerk reaction to temperature increase is to see the symptom as the disease and medicate to bring the temperature back to a level that is 'normal'. When that has been achieved, the problem will seem to be 'gone'. When health isn't measured, how do you know whether bringing the temperature down is a good thing or not? The answer to that question is, you don't. So why is it done? And the answer to that question is, if you can control something (temperature) and bring it back to 'normal', then once that happens the patient is 'measurably' no longer ill.

The point is unless the health of a patient is measured

before and after bringing down the temperature, it is impossible to know whether it is a good idea or not. Our fear of anything not normal blinds us.

Money

When you fight the body with 'anti-medicine', the symptoms may disappear but the health of the patient gets worse and will then require more medicine and more doctoring. More medicine and more doctoring requires more money and this is what we see in Western medicine. More and more money is required to just stay still. More hospitals are required and new expensive drugs are required. There is no end to the amount of money the National Health Service in the UK, for example, will require. Politicians have limited resources and so it will always appear that the practitioners in the NHS are under paid. It will always feel like this. The solution is to get people healthier but you can only do that with the life force.

Many people think that alternative medicine is the use of different remedies or potions that haven't been properly tested. It isn't. Alternative medicine is about employing an alternative *philosophy*.

The Boulderstone Technique is an alternative health system with an alternative philosophy.

What is an alternative philosophy?

Western medicine wants to remove symptoms. If it does this then science deems it effective. If its side effects aren't too damaging then it is called safe.

An alternative philosophy is understanding that the body is always trying to do its best to get back to health, in the most efficient way. The symptoms it produces are in some way helpful and removing them won't help the health of the patient. In fact, as we have shown, purely removing a symptom actually gets in the way of recovery. When you look behind that symptom and ask why is there a distortion in the flow of life force, you might find the real problem. This is using an alternative way of looking at the problem.

Take eczema for example. The standard treatment for eczema is steroid cream. Steroids speed the recovery of the skin but have never cured any case of eczema and yet they are still prescribed. When you employ an alternative way of looking at things, the treatment radically changes.

If the skin is seen for what it is, an organ of elimination, then when the skin tries to excrete something that can't easily pass through the skin, then the skin might become itchy and inflamed and eczema could be diagnosed. The focus shifts from the symptom (itchy skin) to the cause (what's being eaten that the skin is trying to excrete).

Putting anything on the skin surface would be seen as a fruitless way to cure, even if it does eliminate the symptoms for a while. Looking at things in an alternative way is alternative health. In my practice I constantly see that eczema gets worse if people eat dairy products and gets better if people stop eating dairy products. Some doctors are beginning to catch on but dairy products don't affect everyone in the same way. Looking at the cause of a problem is far superior, and cheaper, than dealing with the results but it requires more thought.

Dealing with symptoms and ignoring causes gives instant results but doesn't solve the problem. This myopic philosophy doesn't just pervade healthcare but can also be seen in other 'living' areas such as politics.

Health of the whole

Western medicine is based on pharmaceutical products. The pharmaceutical companies say, 'This medicine works and therefore it is of benefit to the patient.' And by that they mean it sometimes removes or partially removes a symptom. But I believe that the medicine is only of benefit to the patient if it increases the health of that patient. Somewhere along the way Western medical scientists thought that 'this medicine works' was equivalent to 'this medicine will make you healthier', and that is because they didn't measure the health of a patient before and after taking any medicine and instead focused on the symptoms.

The body is always doing the best it can. Even with horrendous symptoms this is still usually the best the body is capable of doing in that moment. Best means best, it doesn't mean that with medicine it can do better.

It isn't that the *illness* is producing the symptoms, it's that the body is functioning according to the flow of life force.

Western medicine goes out of its way to stop whatever the body is naturally trying to do. And every time it does it messes up. Just like it did when deploying DDT.

The same is true with every natural system in the body or in the world at large. For example, remove all mosquitoes and malaria won't go away AND IT WILL CAUSE ANOTHER, BIGGER PROBLEM. Until you totally understand the whole of a system, tinkering with one link in the chain ignores the thousands of years that went into developing the chain and you will inevitably create a problem. Mosquitoes are infected with malaria; it doesn't originate with them. It found a home that led it to proliferate via humans and other animals. You might suppress malaria for a while but it will inevitably bounce back and be more serious.

Believing that symptoms are the illness leads to a failure in health.

Health only lies in the still point.

Getting better

It is impossible to predict precisely how cure will play out and so, when I am working, I don't aim for a particular solution other than a still point. The patient always finds their own path to health. It is always the easiest and most brilliant thing. In a way, I don't do anything. I stay in a still point even though that is not always easy. Perhaps the rearrangement of life force flow will allow the patient to express their previously held-in feelings about how their problem came about or something else will happen. I never have to worry about it because when the restriction is removed whatever happens will result in a healthier outcome.

Every restriction/I-force that is removed is a step towards a still point and health for the patient and, in fact, the whole world. Every time a restriction/I-force is created the opposite is true with a movement toward ill-health.

This points to a definition of healing: healing is a movement towards a still point and illness a movement away.

'Everything should be made as simple as possible, but not simpler' - Albert Einstein

Definition of health

Health is being 'clear', at a still point, where there are no restrictions. Health doesn't come from what happens outside of ourselves. At least, the restrictions that are caused by external factors don't *have* to cause us problems; it is only our reactions to those problems that cause us to claim illness.

Health is the state when we are free from internal restrictions. All these restrictions come from our I-force; they might feel real but they disappear in the face of a still point.

Because they are of our own making, restrictions can always be cleared by the life force using the I-force to point us in the right direction. While all illnesses may be cleared with a still point it doesn't mean we will never die or hurt or suffer but it does mean it is *possible* to be at peace.

Definition of illness

Illness is when we can't get to peace or a still point. Symptoms are our body's attempt to show us the cause of our illness.

Definition of disease

A disease is a fixed list of symptoms diagnosed by a doctor.

Definition of healing

When we follow the life force and don't get diverted by our restrictions, we heal ourselves. And the interesting thing is when another person joins us on that journey the problem is shared and made much easier. It is possible for the journey to health to include using I-force, pills, drugs or surgery but every journey to health must include a following of the life force towards peace.

5

Battles · **Life** · **Symptoms** · **ILLNESS** · **INNER** · **Basis**

Chapter 5: Inner battles - the basis of illness

All symptoms may be *caused* by a distortion in the flow of life force but what keeps them in place? Especially as there is a natural tendency for the life force to play out and heal without any effort on our part. This chapter explains how we end up with symptoms that don't go away.

We get better on our own (if we don't get in the way)

Most illnesses are short-lived and self-limiting, only lasting a few days. However, some illnesses become chronic and settle into a permanent state. There are a number of reasons this happens but they all include some aspect of the illness being ignored by the patient. A common example is the daily consumption of a substance that would only cause a small problem if ingested once a week but can cause a more serious problem when consumed daily. Examples are dairy, tea, coffee, sugar, chocolate and alcohol. Of course, many people can consume these substances daily with little effect. For some people, who have a small problem with them, when they are taken daily and even many times a day can cause chronic symptoms to develop. Some people sense this, even if they haven't been told, which is why they may occasionally fast from them. Most of the time we deny the problems they cause. This denial comes from our I-force, and this can be the foundation of chronic illness.

We fight the healing process

Chronic symptoms occur because our ego gets involved and we ignore the warning signs. It is the same the world over; when we ignore warning signs, our problems will either get worse or we get stuck in a situation that continues. It affects our well-being as well as our health. I get 'messages' all the time from my life force that my ego ignores. 'Do your taxes', 'Check the oil in the car', 'Paint the house', 'Wash some clothes', 'Pay attention', ' Tidy up', 'Eat less sugar', 'Why on earth are you smoking?'. The warnings go away if I do the thing I am meant to, but sometimes I don't and suffer the consequences. Chronic symptoms come about because my ego is adept at listening to my I-force. I have set up a cause for chronic symptoms. And one of the clearest warning symptoms is pain. But what is pain?

Pain and sensation

The level of pain anyone experiences can't be measured with a machine - it is a subjective experience. Unlike other unmeasurable experiences you don't find many scientists saying it doesn't exist. However, it is important to make a distinction between sensation and pain. A sensation is an experience of the body before the ego and I-force get involved. I remember hitting myself on the thumb with a hammer in a typical cartoon-type way, and the sensation was intense. But I managed to just look at the sensation objectively. It was like I wasn't there. It remained a sensation and, for a while at least, it stayed as a sensation and didn't become a pain. I was probably in shock, and my ego wasn't functioning. It took a few more seconds and the sensation turned to pain. But I was left with a question, can all pain be side-lined and become a sensation, and if it does remain a sensation, how does that affect the progress of it getting better?

Sensation is an experience of the body not interpreted by the mind or ego. Sensations can be intense but, in themselves, are neither pleasant nor unpleasant. Those sensations aren't painful; they just are. It is only at the moment we give them a designation that they become a symptom. Whether they are painful or not, once they become a symptom and have an ego and I-force involvement, they become something you want to get rid of and probably with an anti-medicine, such as a painkiller.

Getting back to my thumb, as I said, it didn't take too long before the sensation turned into pain and at that point it became a symptom. Something in me had interpreted the sensation and declared it pain, probably to stop me from doing it again. In the long term that might be helpful. The moment my ego got involved and declared the sensation painful, the I-force became involved and tried to stop the pain.

When any sensation is felt, we have a choice. We can try to suppress it or accept it. With difficult or strong sensations, we often both try to suppress part of it and also accept part of it. These choices govern what will happen next. The ideal solution is to accept it because then nothing gets stuck. This is what happens with mundane occurrences such as stubbing your toe or getting a small splinter. It is rare for these pains to get stuck and for the I-force to get involved. If we told another person about it we might call it pain, but if we kept it to ourselves and didn't tell anyone we might not label it. (To talk to another person we generally involve our ego.)

When in a still point, pain moves to sensation. When I reject strong sensation and want to run away from it and abandon the still point, the sensation becomes pain. Pain hurts, sensation just is. When in a still point all suffering disappears. This is the end of a dance.

When your mind gets traumatised by an experience and you are in pain, there is only one solution. There may be many therapies that try to play out that solution but they all are trying to do the same job. That job is to re-live the trauma in every aspect and at the same time maintain an awareness of the still point. That is the only way. When that has been achieved you will be able to look at any aspect of what happened and not fly off into panic or fear or any other emotion. Every therapy tries to do this except the ones that try to bury or divert from the problem and these avoidance therapies store up problems for the future and should be avoided. (See Chapter 7 on clearing trauma)

When the event or sensation starts to become overwhelming, the I-force gets involved. Someone might scream, swear or cling to someone else in an attempt to suppress the sensation so that the person can still function. During this time, the I-force has to keep working to suppress what is happening, taking energy from its owner. All the time this life force/I-force battle is in progress, there is an inner contradiction, an inner battle. Whenever the I-force is involved, even if it is helping a situation, there is an inner battle, a desire to sort out a situation and also, at the same time, an equal desire to suppress it. This inner battle keeps the symptoms in place and suppresses healing.

Inner battles (I-force vs life force) aren't entirely stable. The mind and body would always prefer a still point where no effort is required. An inner battle is always trying to get resolved, slowly letting out the distortion in the flow of life force, which is why it produces symptoms. The symptoms are pointers to show you the way to solve the inner battle. Unfortunately, Western medicine chooses to see them as something that needs to be stopped and prescribes anti-medicine. Most people work this out subconsciously or even consciously and have a dislike of medication. They often forget to take the tablets or work hard at 'coming off' their tablets.

Suppression

An inner battle is the I-force fighting the life force but in doing so it creates a dance of symptoms. And when the I-force manages to keep back the life force, *chronic* symptoms develop. Examples are many, individual and varied. They can include: stopping yourself from crying when you see something kind happening; or stopping yourself from getting angry at a perceived injustice; or just not knowing how to deal with your own emotions. These situations could easily cause high blood pressure, for example, as the I-force opposes the life force.

Another example of an inner battle leading to a chronic condition could occur from not knowing how to deal with a trauma. After a trauma, the life force wants you to re-live the trauma, so you can come out the other side and not get stuck but the I-force wants to shut the re-living down because it doesn't want to go through that again. The I-force believes it is too much to handle. This is an inner battle. It isn't the trauma alone that causes Post-Traumatic Stress Disorder (PTSD); it is the I-force reaction to the trauma that is the problem. If the inner battle isn't resolved it will lead to a chronic situation.

Chronic pain and trying to live

As soon as the life force stops being distorted (by the I-force) the illness disappears. It is the I-force that keeps our problems in place. Symptoms are the body's way of communicating with you and saying there is a distortion in the flow of life force.

Recap

The cause of every symptom and illness is a distortion in the flow of life force. This distortion is caused, and held in place, by an inner battle. Inner battles are created both consciously and unconsciously but, regardless of how they are created, they are always created by the patient. It doesn't matter how old the patient is; both newborn and geriatric people do this. When anyone is overwhelmed, the overwhelm gets to distort the flow of life force. The only solution that will end in a cure is to remove the distortion. If a distortion remains, so will your symptoms, the symptoms aren't the problem. When you get well, the symptoms aren't needed; removing the symptoms DOESN'T improve the health of the person. Putting steroid cream on an eczema rash may remove the rash until the cream is stopped, which is when the rash returns. The health of the person wasn't improved by the cream; only by clearing the distortion does the health improve.

Consciously created inner battles

Inner battles can occur when you do something you know you shouldn't but you do it anyway. For example, feigning illness to take a day off work, stealing something that doesn't belong to you or lying to a friend.

If the conflict that the ego creates isn't resolved, it will result in an illness. *The purpose of the illness is to undo the conflict.* However, perhaps you can internally justify feigning an illness to take a day off work by saying something like 'I have worked hard on that project and now that it is finished I deserve a day off.' If that justification undoes the internal conflict then no illness will result.

You can also justify lying to a friend by saying something like, 'It is better for them if they don't know the truth.' Again, if the justification works for you, no illness will result. (Lying always requires an inner battle, though.)

Consciously created inner battles point to the existence of the part of you that wants to fight the life force, the ego. The ego, as I see it, is the part of you that resists being thought of as inferior. It is the part that when it gets told to shut up, gets louder. It is the part that marches across the Sahara desert when told it can't. It is also the part that wants to hide under the duvet when the morning alarm goes off. Everyone has one, everyone fights it, and occasionally we win, but sometimes we lose. It isn't separate from us, it is us. But there is a difference between the ego and the part that knows to do the healthy thing - the life force. In a battle between your ego and life force, the life force can always win. However, the ego will put up with a lot of pain and even die trying to show it is better than the life force. It isn't.

Unconsciously created inner battles

Sometimes, an inner battle is created unconsciously by having ideas that seem reasonable within themselves, but when they come together with other equally reasonable ideas they can oppose each other. For example, being an ethical vegan and wearing leather shoes or voting for a political party that then does something you don't agree with. All the ideas are reasonable but, when they come together, they can be in conflict. If these opposing ideas are accepted by your personality they pull in opposing directions and can easily cause depression. (See Chapter 7: Depression)

An unconsciously created inner battle is still an inner battle and needs to be resolved; it creates a disorder in the flow of life force and symptoms, which, as we now know, are pointers to removing the inner battle and clearing distortion.

Having reasonable ideas, which end up opposing each other and leading to depression, is solely caused by the ego of the patient. However, blaming the person who is ill for creating their problem is absurd. If you believe a person wants to be ill you haven't understood illness. Nobody, absolutely nobody, wants to be ill, ever. Those people who you think want to be ill have a bigger problem than you can see.

Anyone can have an inner battle

Children tend to have less fixed views than adults, which is probably why they recover quickly from illnesses and are often more robust. But children can still have fixed views that can lead to inner battles, distortion in the flow of life force and symptoms. If they sort out their problems quickly, without getting overwhelmed, they will go on into adulthood without difficulty. Problems can arise when adults don't tell them the truth about the way things are, in a skilful manner.

For example, children under 3 are generally not aware of what being dead means. Their first experience of death may be in the form of a dead pet, a dead animal by the side of the road or a dead grandparent. When they first become aware of death it is a new concept and, if it isn't explained properly, can cause an inner battle. I don't know the way to explain death to everyone because everyone is different and everyone needs to find their way. I do know lots of ways to explain death badly, though, because I see them in my clinic. Health anxiety is a typical reaction of someone told that anyone can die at any time. While this may be true, it leaves children looking around every corner for something that will kill them and is probably not very helpful.

Children and babies can easily have inner battles which explain night terrors, tantrums, involuntary tics and other fears and anxieties. Those battles can come from being left in hospital without adequate explanation or left in the dark when going to sleep or being left in a school or being vaccinated or other 'medical' procedures and even just from being told 'no'.

Illness comes about from a distortion in the flow of life force. A distortion in the flow of life force comes about through an inner battle.

Beliefs

Causes of inner battles come exclusively from beliefs. Everyone's beliefs are only partially true. Otherwise, they wouldn't be beliefs. For example, the belief that nothing happens after your death leaves your ego wondering what is the point of anything. And the belief that you go on to another life makes your ego not care so much for this one. The good thing about beliefs is that there is a limited number of ways they are created.

When you believe something that isn't an absolute truth, somewhere the opposite will also be true and so there is a conflict. But what is 100% true? What makes something true isn't what another person says, in person or in a religious book or even if everyone says it is. What makes it true is that it doesn't distort your flow of life force. This might sound like a circular argument but not having a distortion in the flow of life force is a very special state and moves you to peace and away from chronic illness, into a still point and out of the dance. (See Chapter 6)

Inner battles are the basis of all illnesses. They are the basis of all mental illness. The arguments we all have with another aspect of ourselves only go quiet when we touch on the peace at the centre of our being. That peace is always there, but it might get overlaid with a partial truth or belief. Inner battles can always be resolved regardless of what has happened to get it there in the first place. We can always get better, regardless of what we believe or what we have done.

Resolving inner battles

Resolving inner battles can be done in many ways but the Boulderstone Technique is the most direct way I have found, as described in this book and outlined here.

The Boulderstone Technique resolves inner battles by tuning into the patient's life force and bringing forward the resistance to the life force that is causing the difficulty. By allowing the energy to move through the body, as it wants to, the inner battle is resolved.

When any inner battle is resolved, the illness that resulted from that inner battle instantly disappears. That includes chronic illness and severe illness.

The purpose of symptoms is to point to where the inner contradiction is

Every inner battle causes a lessening of your vitality. Check it out for yourself. Set up a situation where you have an inner battle. It can be quite mundane: think of something you need to do and at the same time don't want to do. One example might be: I need to clean my windows and I don't want to clean my windows. Make it real and you will feel the tension. The little inner fight you set up drains you of a small piece of vitality. Not enough to trigger an illness but then it is only about window dirt.

The (small) lack of vitality is the illness and if you study the feeling you will see that it directly points back to the cause: the inner battle between wanting clean windows and not wanting to clean them. The point of symptoms is to help you to resolve inner conflict. The solution is to resolve the inner contradiction and the solutions to that are many. You could wash the windows. You could smash the windows, they then wouldn't need cleaning. You could learn to live with them. You could poke your eyes out. Every one of those ideas resolves that small inner contradiction and will remove the associated lack of vitality. It may cause another inner battle but it will remove the original inner battle. The way you resolve the inner battle is your business but the symptoms are the pointers to the problem. Covering over the symptoms with any medication or distraction keeps the problem in place with the need for stronger symptoms.

The size of the inner battle is dependent only on the patient not on the act

I have met quite a few people who have killed another person and the conflict within them may be large or small, depending on the way *they* view it.

Of three people who killed separate people, one was awake most nights pacing his room, talking to himself in a very agitated state. His inner contradiction was great and it affected him in the mental sphere. He was only going to get to peace through believing in a higher power. If he couldn't he would probably go mad, if he wasn't already. I met him on a meditation retreat in a darkened cave where he stayed for 30 days. I believe he was trying to blank out or isolate his thoughts.

Another person who had killed someone had been diagnosed with Multiple Sclerosis (MS). I feel I understand people diagnosed with MS (see MS section, Chapter 7) in that they all use tension in their neck and body to stop their emotions from getting out of control. In my view, MS is an emotional illness where the patient has discovered a way of dealing with unresolved emotional difficulties by clamping down on them and simulating peace and a still point. Unfortunately, in my opinion, this leads to clamping down on their nerves with the typical MS symptoms following. The solution to MS is to resolve the inner battle, what else? (More on MS in Chapter 7)

And yet another person who had killed someone seemed to be not too bothered by what they did.

The level of disturbance is based solely on the patient's internal battle and nothing else.

(All three people were from the armed forces and the killings were considered legal.)

Other ways inner battles come about

Even looking at planet Earth there can be conflicting views. Wanting to look after the planet and taking one or two flights a year for a holiday are two ideas that individually might seem reasonable but together might create a conflict. The problem is that if we hold both of those views they will make our perfect mind less than perfect.

Inner contradiction doesn't just come from passive views about the world. Sometimes circumstances occur that will create a big inner battle. Usually, these come about in violent ways. A car accident, for example, could cause the physical body to be pulled in different directions. This is physical conflict which can cause ongoing discomfort, such as whiplash. A thought that might come up during the accident is 'I don't want to die' but the truth of it is, in the end, we all die. It will bring up the problem every one of us has about death. If we haven't sorted out that issue beforehand there is bound to be a conflict.

Conflict could arise days after the accident. For example, if another person was seriously injured in the accident the question might come into your head 'That should have been me, why did I escape unhurt?' Inner battles will develop without much effort on our part.

Inner battles are only created by the individual affected

The point is, all inner battles are created by the individual experiencing them. It is the world view of the individual that is wholly responsible, regardless of the circumstance or even age or intellectual ability of the person. One way of understanding this is to realise that, regardless of the situation, not everyone is affected in the same way. The person who knows how to resolve inner battles will walk away from any difficulty without any mental or emotional conflicts because they are at peace and will consequently recover quickly.

Western medicine practitioners generally dislike this idea, that the level of illness is created by the patient. WM wants to absolve everyone of their illnesses so that it can give them pills which will clear up their symptoms. How have we got ourselves into this position of not taking responsibility for the way we react to events?

Inner battles that come from opposing views have to be either held in place or resolved. In the perfect mind the inner contradiction is always resolved and resulting problems go away but if the fight is held in place then it will always reduce vitality because it takes energy to avoid dealing with problems. Even knowing this doesn't always help, I still procrastinate when it comes to doing my tax return because a part of me believes if I put it off I will save myself some pain. Of course, I am wrong.

Even when the conflict is held the mind will try to get it resolved, sometimes waiting until you are relaxed or in a deep sleep and your defences are lowered. This is why panic attacks can appear to come from out of the blue when least expected and also why bad dreams can occur.

Resolving inner battles brings you closer to the perfect mind but often requires you to re-live an incident that contributed to the formation of the conflict. This is where remembered-pain (as opposed to direct-pain) comes to the surface. Remembered pain is not really pain and it is unfortunate that it is called pain. Most physical pain exists to get you to move away from its cause and remember to stay away. To clear remembered pain you have to go into it and feel it completely, bringing yourself to a still point at the same time as remembering the pain. Once this has been achieved the pain part of the remembered pain disappears. Embarrassment is a form of remembered pain that can be removed by this process, leaving the memory intact but without the uncomfortable feeling.

Without inner battles we are clear and free from anxiety, embarrassment and confusion. With inner contradiction we often don't even know what we want. This is because when we connect with the conflict, our thoughts and feelings follow the paths of the two conflicting ideas and can move off in different directions. When opposing views collide we end up confused or anxious or both. Doctors, for some reason, are adept at creating these opposing views in their patients. Perhaps because it is easy to do. All they have to say is 'I don't like the look of that lump, but you can't have a scan for a couple of weeks.' Or 'I can give you an appointment in six months.'

Satisfactorily resolving the conflict isn't something we are taught. Especially if our parents didn't know how. Television dramas rely on their characters not knowing how to resolve conflict. As a teaching medium television is second to none, it just teaches how not to solve problems. Also we are taught from an early age to actively avoid physical and emotional pain. But resolving emotional pain requires us to seek it out. Instead, we are taught to avoid all pain often with pharmaceutical drugs. Even our friends will say, 'Have a cup of tea/coffee/cigarette/drink/etc'.

Drugs distract
Drugs only rarely solve the inner contradiction problem

but they are seductive in that they can distract you. Most drugs distract. Indeed, that is my definition of a drug: a substance that puts you into a different mindset. Legal recreational drugs like alcohol, tea, coffee and tobacco all put you into a slightly different mind set. That is their purpose. If you need to change the way you are thinking then they are the substance for you. Sugar, television and reading all can do the same but are not as reliable and therefore weaker. Stronger drugs, like heroin, cocaine and their derivatives, are stronger because they are more reliable in putting you into a different mind set. None of them solves the problem.

Projecting inner contradiction

One way people try to resolve inner battles is to project the conflict outwards and find the problem in their outer world. Picking an argument with someone when the real argument is with yourself is very common. There will always be a problem in the external world that is close enough to the problem in your inner world to draw you in.

I have seen people who engage in politics because they want control. They seek power probably because they feel weak. They may become a doctor if they dislike being ill or become a teacher if they want to learn. They are all ways people try to resolve their inner battles by projecting them outwards. Unfortunately, it is an inefficient method of healing and generally people get lost, forget why they started and, as a result, often burn out. Externalising our inner battles is a way of not taking full responsibility for our conflicts. I spent nearly thirty years learning this lesson.

I now believe it is better to sort out my inner world before trying to sort out our outer world. I argue that it is only when you are free of inner contradiction that the changes you make in the outer world will be authentic and acceptable to others.

'First remove the beam out of your own eye, and then you can see clearly to remove the speck out of your brother's eye' - Matthew 7:5, The Bible

---

When you are free from inner battles certain things happen:

- You become your own person: you live an authentic life
- You see the true value of things
- You know how you are responsible for your life.
- Self-improvement happens automatically: you don't need to seek it out.
- Life decisions become easy: you know that peace is the answer.
- You don't experience anxiety: you are healthy, you sleep like a baby.

It is probable that everyone has experienced these things for at least a short time but it is the depth of experience that defines freedom from contradiction. Feeling like this for a few minutes is helpful but it is possible to feel like this for days on end and longer.

Maintaining a mind free from contradiction

A mind free from contradiction and battles is something that can be extended and deepened by one's actions and behaviours. One of the easiest ways to extend and deepen the experience is by meditation (See Chapter 9 and Appendix: Meditation). Every action that comes from peace generates a situation where peace is more easily available.

Meditation and your life's purpose

People often ask me for help in finding their true purpose in life because they believe that everyone has a purpose. I don't know whether everyone has a purpose or not but I know how to find it if you have one. Meditation is not about keeping your mind quiet but about being aware of everything that comes up in your thoughts and feelings and processing them to get back to peace. You know that if someone is annoying you that punching their lights out is going to leave you with more inner contradiction not less and so you look around for other ways to keep your mind free. If you look you will find one; it will always be personal to you and it will be your purpose.

When you manage to keep your mind free from contradiction you will automatically be following your life purpose. It is unique to you and it is dynamic, meaning it changes as you change. Everything else takes you to inner contradiction and ill health. If you can manage to sit around all day not doing anything, without inner contradiction, then you are doing the right thing for you, although sitting all day is harder than most people think. Keeping a perfect mind is the very opposite of boring; you have to be adaptable in every situation.

All illness, physical and mental, can be permanently removed when you know the real cause of the illness. The problem with modern Western medicine is that its focus on symptom removal blocks the pointers that are showing you the way forward. No wonder people have lost their way.

Where do bacteria and viruses fit in?

Germ theory remains a cornerstone of Western medicine, explaining how infectious diseases are spread through microorganisms like bacteria and viruses.

However, this understanding doesn't paint the whole picture. Many bacteria and viruses coexist peacefully with us, even benefiting our health.

Western medicine relies heavily on Germ Theory to explain how infectious diseases spread. This has led to a view of bacteria and viruses as enemies to be eradicated and is probably the reason antibiotics are so freely given by doctors. However, the reality is more complex. While some microbes cause illness, others play vital roles in our health. Indeed without them, we would die.

Examples of helpful viruses

Some helpful viruses are bacteriophages. These viruses are abundant in the environment and play a crucial role in controlling bacterial populations. Endogenous retroviruses are viruses integrated into our DNA and have become part of our genome, providing us with essential functions. Some common cold viruses can cause mild discomfort but many others are harmless and even help train our immune systems to fight off possible future infections. Some human papillomaviruses (HPVs) can cause warts or cancer but most HPV strains are harmless and don't cause any symptoms.

Also, some bacteria are positively good for us, helping us to digest food, protecting us from disease-causing microbes, and some even produce vitamins and other nutrients. The same is true for some viruses, fungi and protozoa.

Everyone reacts differently

It is important to note that bacteria and viruses that cause symptoms don't always do so in a consistent manner, especially outside a laboratory. Human beings react differently to the same bug. For instance, the Epstein-Barr virus infects about 95% of people worldwide by the time they reach the age of 50. While most people don't experience any symptoms, some may have life-threatening symptoms. Furthermore, people who live in the same house and catch the 'same' cold can have vastly different symptoms. Some may experience throat-related symptoms, while others may have nose-related or lung-related symptoms. It is apparent that there is more to the disease than just the presence of a particular microbe.

Of course, Western medical scientists will tell you the difference is in the immune system but they do not factor in the I-force. A factor that can have an effect before the immune system gets a look in.

The I-force reaction is significant

We already know that a cause of stress is a life force/I-force battle AND that both acute and chronic stress directly affect the immune system. Therefore, the I-force is a factor in the functioning of the immune system. So, a strong I-force could be responsible for the Epstein-Barr virus having a small or large negative effect. The point is the state of the I-force is an important factor in whether you become ill or not.

Theory, theory everything theory

Germ Theory says that bacteria and viruses directly cause disease. Although Germ Theory has been strongly adopted by Western medicine it is not yet fact. There is another unproven theory that suggests that microbes exploit existing weaknesses in the body's internal environment. Not a theory that pharmaceutical companies would want to support. My theory is that those weaknesses stem from internal conflicts, a life force/I-force battle, and microbes, in exploiting these weaknesses, show us what needs to be addressed.

What happens to get you ill?

Before showing any symptoms there is always a palpable distortion in the flow of life force. That is not theory but what I feel in my practice. This distortion could have been created minutes before or years before symptoms emerge. It could have come from a trauma or an incident where the ego was challenged but, whatever the cause, the I-force comes into effect and there is a life force/I-force battle. At this point, there are even a few minor warning signs depending on the cause of the distortion. To get ill the person has to ignore the warning signs. If they didn't ignore them, and instead did something about them, the illness wouldn't progress in the same way. The life force/I-force battle creates a blind spot that allows a microbe a home and creates subsequent symptoms.

In finding a home the microbe can go wild, exceeding its boundaries, causing symptoms and even a diagnosable disease, until it is detected and stopped. The real problem is the I-force that got in the way. Killing off the microbe might stop the symptoms but it doesn't sort out the I-force or the problem.

When something is true on one level there is often a parallel truth on a different level.

The situation at the microbe level is also played out at a macro level.

The basis of every soap opera storyline is the life force/I-force battle being played out. At a basic level one character does something but hides their actions from another character and tension is built up. The tension is the life force/I-force battle that produces symptoms or, in this case, drama. The 'illness' is really the life force/I-force battle but the 'symptoms' will continue until the illness is resolved.

On another level …

It seems to me that politicians are often on the lookout for easy solutions to problems and are more likely to solve society's symptoms than deal with causes. Rounding up homeless people doesn't solve the problem of how they got there in the first place. Taxing carbon dioxide output won't stop global warming and stopping people from smoking won't stop teenagers' desire to experiment with risky behaviours.

Money

A huge amount of money is in play when we are talking about symptom removal and there could well be a vested interest in the relevant industries keeping the status quo. A way to change this situation is not to litigate against pharmaceutical companies for putting profits above people's health. This is just a version of symptom removal. Instead, the change comes from dealing with the cause and that cause is the belief that symptoms are the problem. How do you do that? You connect with your own life force. It is as simple as that.

What to do

Microbes are often found at the scene of an illness but being found at the scene doesn't mean the microbe is the cause of the illness. Bacteria and viruses can certainly create symptoms but they were let in. We live with bacteria and viruses in our environment all the time but they only become a problem under certain conditions. Those conditions are connected to the life force and I-force.

While medicine might kill off the bacteria or virus and temporarily relieve symptoms, it often doesn't address the cause of the illness. I believe this root cause lies in a distortion in the flow of life force. While I can't scientifically prove this, and perhaps I never will, the lack of scientific proof doesn't automatically make something untrue. My experience shows that working with life force and removing distortions in its flow provides genuine, lasting help for people – far beyond simply managing their symptoms.

Following the life force and allowing it to dismantle the I-force uncovers a still point that was always there. That still point which can exist in yourself and in the wider world, is devoid of symptoms and illness. And all you have to do to achieve this health is connect with your own life force.

Summary

The purpose of symptoms is to point to our inner contradiction.

Dance

Still point

Mind

6

Chapter 6: The Mind Dance and the Still Point

When there are no inner battles and you KNOW something is true, there is no debate. You know it from the bottom of your heart. (Your ego, however, wanting to have this ability, will often get in the way and try to copy this feeling so that sometimes your 'knowing' comes from the heart of your bottom and is incorrect.)

When KNOWING is accurate, the feeling is that the knowledge is pure and you might even say that knowledge 'comes from God'. All I know is some truths exist internally, are there before language and are independent of language. In this situation there is no inner battle. However, the Tower of Babel story from the Bible taught us that as soon as you speak those truths, by turning them into a language, the language changes them and they instantly gain an inner contradiction. They become relative truths, dependent on time, space and culture. You feel this for yourself when you wake from a dream knowing something absolutely but unable to express it to another person.

And so we play the mind dance wanting to know and communicate the truth but unable to do so with words. We can get close to understanding the truth of what someone has written, especially if what we read or hear comes from the same or similar culture to us but even then if we take what is written as being absolute truth it will cause us problems. Religious texts are the most difficult. See Appendix: the language of knowing.

The mind dance

There is only one illness: a distortion in the flow of life force. This one illness manifests in all the diseases that exist in the Western medical texts. There are many different ways of removing symptoms with the use of many different pharmaceutical drugs but there is just one way to remove the illness for each person. That one way is personal to the patient and is the main reason Western medical drugs rarely cure, even if they partially remove symptoms.

If there is only one way to remove the distortion in the flow of life force and cure each person, why and how has a multibillion-dollar industry grown up around removing symptoms? The answer to that question lies in our ego. There are people prepared to say 'We know better than the body and can remove this particular symptom with our expensive drug.' And who doesn't want to get rid of their symptoms?

Pharmaceutical companies employ scientists who aren't paid to look at the whole illness, they are only paid to look at the symptoms. The larger truth is that medicine, while it may reduce symptoms, actually diminishes the health of the people who take it and sometimes can even cause death.

To a certain degree, we are all guilty. What do you do when you have a headache? Do you take a painkiller? I think most people have done so. Looking at the cause of your problem has gained a whole lot of criticism because it is somehow believed you need a counsellor and at least six months of therapy to process your family dynamics, just to resolve your headache.

If there is only one illness why are there so many diseases? Chapter 7 aims to answer that question and looks at groups of symptoms that have been pulled together and defined as a particular disease.

The mind dance and the still point

Being in perfect health requires your mind, emotions and body all to be healthy. Which comes first, mind, body or emotions? By now it should be clear that the life force is the most important. The mind, body and emotions reflect what is going on in the flow of life force, each according to its nature.

When you have a perfect mind, free from inner contradiction and settled in the still point, a healthy body without illness will follow. Health, both mental and physical, is only dependent on the flow of life force. Whenever you think something isn't healthy that is because something isn't healthy.

There is no other definition of perfect health other than being able to sit in a still point. So it is possible to be healthy and only have one leg, or have any other disability, as long as you can rest in a still point. Whenever someone has any symptom, be it physical, mental or emotional, there will be an inner contradiction and battle behind it and a distortion in the flow of life force. When that inner contradiction is cleared so is the physical, mental or emotional symptom. If someone has one leg and no inner contradiction they will have no issue with their body. Their body will be perfect for them. It isn't the state of the body that determines health but the state of the flow of life force.

Your body/mind is always trying to clear whatever inner contradiction you may have, but if you don't listen, the only resource it has to get you to listen is to 'turn up the volume' and increase the number or intensity of your symptoms. Symptoms aren't bad things to be removed. Even though they feel like they are, especially if you ignored the earlier signs. Instead, they are pointers in the direction of how you can get better. Ignore them or medicate them and your health will suffer. Luckily, your body/mind will keep trying to get you better even if you do try to medicate them; it just takes longer.

Questions about health, then, always come down to:

'How do I complete this dance and rest in a still point?'

Health lies in a still point and the only way to get there is to allow your life force to take you there, in the same way a stream will find its easiest course. When you are at peace you 'know' it. When you aren't at peace or are 'in the dance' you only sometimes know it.

A still point is our natural state; it is only when we are 'in the dance' that we are (sometimes) aware something isn't right. We all learn how to get to a still point through baby steps and we start learning probably even before we are born. As we rest in our mother's womb, her state of mind is intimately connected with our own. Mothers teach their babies to rest in the still point just by placing their hands on their bump and connecting or tuning in. It happens naturally and can be seen wherever there are pregnant people. This is love and that baby is learning about that love. A still point is love.

After the baby is born, whenever it settles into peace and sleeps, it is usually in a still point. Whenever there is a problem and it is 'in the dance', it makes a noise that is difficult to ignore. It is trying to find its way back to the still point. Through this process, if we are lucky, we begin to learn what a still point is and isn't and we continue to use that information throughout our lives.

When you are in a real still point, there is nothing to tell you, you are there. If you had a voice in your head that told you that you were in a still point that voice would be part of the dance and would be proof you are still in the dance. The still point just is; no machine, doctor, priest or person can force you into one.

Moving To A Still Point

Being in the middle of a crisis is the most difficult time

to try and learn how to move to a still point. The time to learn how still points work is when there is only a small disturbance, like when you have a tune stuck in your head and you want it out, for example. Understanding how you get rid of the tune is a good way to learn how to get to the still point because it is the same method you use to get rid of anxiety, trauma, guilt, grief, a bad memory and even hiccoughs.

There are many methods of removing an unwanted tune from your head. You can do it with drugs. You can shock it out. You can replace it with another tune. Or you can process the need for it.

Burnout and stress

Burnout is set up by the inner contradiction: I have to do this ~ I don't want to do this. The longer you force yourself and the more you force yourself the greater the burnout. The longer you keep it up without resolving it the worse it becomes. The pressures of believing you have to do something often come from a job where there are high expectations. In the UK, that often means doctors, nurses, police officers, prison officers, teachers and social workers but of course burnout isn't restricted to these professions. Burnout can be created by unresolved stress in any job.

Just about the worst thing Western medical doctors do in this situation is to prescribe drugs. Drugs will never resolve burnout and stress and will only make it harder to resolve. Probably the second worst thing Western medicine does is believe that counselling is the way to sort out unresolved, emotional issues. Talking, in itself, can't resolve a distortion in the flow of life force. However, for some people, it might help by removing some symptoms.

Doctors in the UK probably think: I haven't got time to

help this person so who can I pass them on to? I am convinced their thinking often doesn't go beyond that thought. Stress is always and only caused by the person who experiences it. Of course, people can put pressure on you that can translate into stress but it is only the patient who creates the stress. Stress comes from having a conscience and wanting to do a good job, sometimes a job that isn't even possible. Here lie clues to the inner contradiction.

Old hands in these difficult jobs manage to survive in a number of ways. Alcohol appears to release difficult thoughts, although it is only a temporary solution. Prescription drugs are given by doctors who feel they can't do anything else. These always make the situation worse which is why some patients reject them. Not caring anymore is another solution but creates a deeper distortion. But there is a way to eliminate burnout and stress efficiently, quickly and painlessly without talking or taking medication. I explain how we remove stress in chapter 7.

You are your best diagnostician

When a person says they are not well but have no symptoms, Western medics can't do anything except perform tests. If the tests come back negative, does that mean that the person is healthy? Not necessarily. When something is wrong the patient feels it as a distortion in their flow of life force. It is always real. When a person is well they are content with their life and would not be asking for sympathy or attention.

It is so important to listen to the patient. If they can feel something is wrong how difficult is it to have them lie on a couch, hold their head and ask them to feel the sensation that tells them they aren't well? A Boulderstone Technique practitioner can feel what is happening in the patient. There is a Western medical worry that the patient might be lying to get attention but isn't this also an illness?

Peace, health and happiness are synonyms. When nothing agitates you then you are at peace, healthy and happy. As soon as something causes you to be upset and peace gets covered over, happiness is lost and your health is compromised. The level of ill health won't be measurable by a machine because there are too many factors but another human being, trained in the Boulderstone Technique, will be able to measure it, compare it to previous levels and know where you are headed. Something can always done because the illness doesn't exist in the external world.

For example, a mother says she is upset because her children have grown up and left the family home. The problem may appear to exist outside of the mother but the real problem is inside her. How do I know? Because some people aren't upset by the same situation. The mother isn't residing in a still point. When she can get there, she will be at peace.

Trauma
ANXIETY
Panic attacks
Life force
Autism
Obsessions
Cancer
Mind
Time
Feel
Symptoms
Process
People
Phobias
Problems
Point
Death

Chapter 7: The dances

This chapter contains my take on diagnosable diseases and illnesses. I do not diagnose these illness and I do not pronounce cure. Instead, I look at the distortion in the flow of life force, find the cause of this distortion and show the patient how to resolve it.

The purpose of this chapter is to show how a distortion in the flow of life force can give rise to many different dances. The I-force and the life force, with their push-pull effects, form these dances and being able to work with these forces is enough to cure all of them. What I mean by cure is to get the patient to process the distortion in the flow of life force. When this distortion is removed the need for the body's messages (symptoms) disappears. I will explain exactly how I do that later in this chapter. Every single dance explained here is susceptible to the same solution albeit in a slightly different form.

The first dance and building block of the other problems is stress. Stress is a self-created dance that appears to come from outside of the person but, in fact, never does. Stress is the archetypal illness. If you understand how it comes about and how to clear it then you can clear trauma, PTSD, panic attacks, anxiety, prolonged grief, obsessions, compulsions, phobias, depression and even multiple sclerosis and more. Stress is the building block of many illnesses.

Stress

Most of the time, most people just put up with their stress. Sometimes, though the stress doesn't go and becomes long term. Short-term stress happens when you face unforeseen events or challenges that disrupt your plans or expectations. The stress comes about because you believe something should be one way but it isn't that way and an inner battle is created. Examples of short-term stress include getting stuck in traffic, losing your keys, receiving an unexpected bill, disagreeing with a loved one, or missing a deadline. All of these stresses may affect your well-being.

The minute you accept the situation, short-term stress disappears. While in the stressful state you will often hear the stressed person say, 'I don't believe it', or 'Is that for real?' Or 'You can't be serious'. All phrases point to the inner battle of not accepting the way things are.

As soon as the situation is accepted the stress disappears. Short-term stress is vulnerable to talking about the situation. Even talking to strangers in the form of counsellors can be helpful because expressing what you think often forces the conflicting thought into a more logical and coherent form and can change your viewpoint.

Long-term stress occurs when short-term stress doesn't get resolved. Long-term stress occurs because you feel you have to fight against the situation you are in. For example, long-term stress could come about through living in a noisy, chaotic or unsafe environment, The stress comes from fighting the perceived situation. It could be being underpaid while struggling to make ends meet, caring for a loved one with a disability or living with a culture of bullying. Each of these stresses appears because you feel you have to fight to just stay stable. These stresses appear to be created by external events but that is not and is never the case. External events exist which can allow you to pin the stress on them but the external events are not the cause. They appear to be the cause but it is always possible to remove the stress without changing the external situation. That is not to say it is acceptable to create a situation to make another person experience stress. Consciously causing another person stress points to a serious illness in the person causing the stress.

Stress removal

One of the first questions I ask someone who comes to me complaining of stress is 'How do you know you are stressed?'

And they generally answer by reeling off their symptoms. Symptoms such as sleeplessness, difficulty breathing, fatigue, headaches, high blood pressure, indigestion and so on. But I say, 'These are the symptoms of stress, they are not what tells you, you are stressed.'

When you look at what tells you, you are stressed it is always the same thing. There is a physical tension somewhere in your body. This tension is caused by an inner battle or contradiction, as explained in Chapter 5. Your mind creates the inner contradiction as a way of holding on to the conflicting viewpoints about yourself without them clashing. The cause of your stress is this tension, not the symptoms.

The solution is the resolving of the tension. Nothing needs to change in the external world for you to be free from stress. Physical exercise can sometimes temporarily remove stress because it resolves the physical tension. Unfortunately, that tension generally comes back quite quickly after experiencing the external 'stressor'.

Once the physical tension that tells the patient they are stressed has been identified and written on the trauma ticket the practitioner is ready to remove this sensation. The sensation is a physical manifestation of their distorted life force. When *this* sensation is processed, they don't feel stressed any more.

The next stage is for the *practitioner* to feel the sensation that causes the stress. When the practitioner connects with the patient and the patient connects with the sensation that tells them they are stressed, the practitioner can also feel it and will know how to process that stress sensation. The sensation isn't just removed, it is processed. The practitioner knows how to do this because that is what they are trained to do.

You process the physical sensation that tells them they are stressed by allowing the sensation to complete its purpose and it returns to a still point. The patient's tendency has been to actively stop that process from happening because stopping it felt better than allowing it to continue its movement. This is the heart of the stress, the inner conflict. However, when they allow the movement to complete and the patient is resting in a still point there is no stress, they are cured. This is a complete and proper cure. No talking is necessary and nothing has to change in the external world. Taking the stress sensation to a still point is all that is necessary. During this process the patient comes to see their inner conflict and resolve it.

You don't need to talk about the contradiction for hours on end and you can probably resolve the stress in ten minutes or less. I have done this for thousands of people and taught hundreds to do it for themselves.

I review this process later in this chapter: Processing an event or trauma.

See for yourself

Let's create a fictitious situation to see how stress affects you and then walk through the process of removing it. First, we need to build the stress. Let's do this with an imaginary bill that unexpectedly arrives. The amount can be of your choice but make it an amount where it makes you catch your breath. This will vary from person to person. Fix the amount and then multiply it by three! Understand you have to pay it off in the next few weeks or something very serious will happen.

Build it up until you can feel the physical tension. Even just using your imagination, you might be able to see how it could be responsible for stress symptoms. Especially if you took sole responsibility for it and were too embarrassed to tell anyone. Imagine walking around with that tension all day preying on your mind. As the days pass the stress becomes greater.

This is the power of the I-force working against your life force. Can you see that if one of your symptoms was sleeplessness taking a sleeping pill would never remove the stress? Or if you have difficulty breathing, a diagnosis of asthma and the consequent inhaler would fail to touch the stress even if it did remove the symptom. The symptoms of sleeplessness or difficulty breathing are pointers to the problem, not the problem itself. Taking a medication that helps the symptom but leaves the stress focusses the problem on the wrong area and stops the person getting better. This is the problem with Western medicine.

Back to the example. So how do you resolve the stress without paying the bill? Paying the bill will relieve the stress but the stress isn't coming from the lack of money, the stress is coming from the interaction of your I-force and life force and that is what needs to change for the stress to go and not come back. Of course, stress can be useful, galvanising you into action, as long as it is short-lived. But I would suggest that if you were going to get something done you would be more efficient if you don't have to also contend with the symptoms of stress. Being tired or worried about your breathing does not make you more efficient. Fear doesn't make you smarter.

The first step in resolving the stress is to find the internal cause. That is why I ask, 'How do you know you are stressed?' I am trying to get the patient to focus on the physical tension that they are using to keep their inner contradiction from clashing. The clashing is their I-force and the life force fighting. In our example, the contradiction is the demand for money and the inability to pay. This battle causes the stress and its resultant symptoms.

My skill, if I have any, is that I have trained myself to feel this inner battle. Practically, it is easier to feel it in another person than it is to feel it in yourself. Being able to feel the life force and I-force battle is key to resolving it in another person, as I will explain in a moment. First I want to talk about stress's big brothers: trauma and PTSD.

Trauma and Post-traumatic Stress Disorder (PTSD)

Trauma occurs when the capacity of the mind to process information is exceeded. Another word for this situation is 'overwhelm'. It happens when the mind is shocked by the amount or quality of information. This can happen quickly or slowly. An example of slowly induced trauma is when a child is neglected by their parents or a person is regularly bullied.

When the overwhelming incident is over, if the trauma processing continues and gets completed, there will be no PTSD but if the processing is stopped before it has finished, conflict in the mind will remain. You and your life force will continue to search for opportunities to fully process the trauma while another part (I-force) will try and stop that from happening. This is the conflict talked about in chapter 5.

These opportunities to process the trauma are places and times that appear safe for the person. The mind then replays the trauma to allow processing of it to complete. This can get called a flashback or panic attack and, unfortunately, is rarely seen as a chance to finish processing the difficult incident because they usually contain too much information, arriving too quickly. Attempts are often made to suppress these panic attacks or flashbacks but this is what keeps them in place. For many, these panic attacks appear to arrive randomly but they don't. They usually occur in a place and at a time when the patient is relaxed and, as far as the limited perception of the mind is concerned, able to complete the task.

Without understanding that traumas need to be processed, treating them with medication, or even counselling, will fail or take an exceedingly long time. Processing must be achieved but it doesn't have to be difficult or painful. The patient doesn't have to repeat their traumatic experience to process the events. Indeed, if they do repeat their traumatic experience and it fails to fully process the patient may end up in a worse state.

If the processing of a traumatic memory isn't completed then the patient will remain in a traumatised state until the memory is processed. Human beings can compartmentalise traumas and can temporarily hide them away. At first sight, this appears to be a good thing because you can get on with your life, saving the problem to be dealt with later. The trauma, though, won't stay in its box. The mind wants to heal it and waits for a time when the person is relaxed and able to complete the task. Whenever the trauma breaks out of its box a panic attack, or similar, will ensue.

If it is contained in its box, the distortion in the flow of life force will eventually transform the mental/emotional problem onto the physical level, possibly as an inflamed joint, encapsulated cyst or tumour. Before this happens there will be indicators that something is wrong and needs to be addressed. Ignoring these messages, or medicating them, will only get the body to 'turn up the volume' and make the symptoms worse so that you listen. Symptoms are your body's way of talking to you. Of course, the mind and body can process events over time, just by letting time pass, but this is generally a slow, passive process. It is better to respond to messages from your body by dealing with them directly.

Processing a traumatic event can be stopped by effort of will, by distraction, by other people, by drugs, including anaesthetic, or by another similar incident. But when it is regularly stopped it becomes a more complex conflict that can be extremely difficult to process.

Trauma can come about for many reasons. I personally only released the trauma from my birth in my thirties but I believe it would have stayed there my whole life if I hadn't identified it and cleared it. At that time, I cleared most of it using a technique called re-birthing. Despite its name re-birthing can be used for releasing any trauma. It is more efficient than talking therapies but it is still not as efficient as the Boulderstone Technique.

To make things worse, traumas can also be caused before birth, either because a trauma occurred to the mother while pregnant or because a medical procedure was performed on the foetus. Talking therapies are of virtually no use here but the distortion in the flow of life force is real, it can be felt by another person, and it can be undone. Proving this scientifically would, however, be a challenge.

I have treated thousands of people with traumas that have occurred in many different ways from the shock of losing a parent or sibling to sexual, emotional or physical abuse, as well as shock from witnessing abuse. Anytime the ability of the mind to process information is exceeded, a trauma can be created. Traumas are often created in hospitals, as a patient or even as a visitor, on battlefields, in road traffic accidents, but also in places like cinemas.

Horror films deliberately try to create a trauma in people because a trauma-inducing film can also be an antidote to a previous similar trauma. This could explain why horror films can become addictive and some people gravitate towards traumas they have already experienced.

Every single trauma that I have described can be felt by another person as a physical sensation, if they know what they are looking for. This is the key to removing PTSD without talking or medication, in a very short time, with a Boulderstone Technique practitioner. And it usually takes less than a day. Complex PTSD can sometimes take two days. If you do not have access to a Boulderstone Technique practitioner you could try to use the technique on yourself. You will find a self-administered version in the Appendix, although I would recommend working by yourself only for simple traumas, and certainly not for complex PTSD.

A distortion in the flow of life force can be felt by a Boulderstone Technique practitioner. What can also be felt is the use of anaesthetic after an operation. It feels like anaesthetic creates gaps in awareness and could be labelled as a negative trauma. Negative traumas are virtually impossible to remove with a talking therapy because the mind finds it difficult to talk about something that doesn't appear to be there. Actually feeling a negative trauma is possible, though, and can be removed using the Boulderstone Technique. Recreational drugs, including alcohol, can fall into this 'anaesthetic' category but can also cause a standard trauma just by poisoning the body. 'Flashbacks' of negative trauma could be spacing out, losing concentration, losing the ability to stay focussed, ADD type symptoms.

Physical trauma

Another form of trauma that can be felt as a distortion in the flow of life force is physical trauma. A case that comes to mind was that of a young dog that was running across a field when it got its foot caught in a rabbit hole. I was quite surprised that the dog hadn't broken its leg, the injury was that severe, but an X-ray had found the bones intact. I saw the animal a few days after the accident when the owner felt the dog should have been improving and it wasn't. I held the foot and felt life force distortion. I allowed the bones to move in the way they wanted to, which was an incredibly difficult thing to do as the dog was certainly in distress. I held firm realising that the pulling away from pain was stopping the injury from getting better. As I followed the life force movement through the pain difficulty we came out the other side and a still point was reached. The dog walked off happy and restored to health.

Having pain can often keep a problem in place, be it mental, emotional or physical. I have since worked on many different physical problems, seeing very stuck problems getting resolved in seconds, usually putting my hands on the injured part of the body. Problems sorted have been strains, sprains, arthritis, dislocations, twists, shingles and even mosquito bites.

Processing a trauma or stress using the Boulderstone Technique

Processing stored traumas, events or stresses is done in the same way. When understood it is simple and usually also easy. The fundamental method also doesn't change from person to person although sometimes minor details may vary.

The first step is to help the person connect with their

trauma internally but not so strongly that they get overwhelmed. In my clinic, this is achieved by asking the patient to think of a single word that represents their trauma, which I write on a piece of paper. I refer to this as 'the trauma ticket'. If you are still holding the trauma from the example above you might write 'bill' on the trauma ticket. During the therapy session, the patient lies on a massage couch and places the trauma ticket on their stomach. Meanwhile, I hold their head. While the trauma ticket is 'on', they connect with the trauma. As they think about the trauma I can feel the distortion in their flow of life force and when I have enough to work with, I say 'off', and the patient takes the trauma ticket off. When the ticket is 'off', they stop thinking about the trauma. The limited amount of gathered trauma is then processed. This process is repeated until there is nothing left to process. If you are still working with the example see how you can get rid of the tension.

Working in this way we have control over the trauma. While the ticket is on the patient, and they are connecting with it, I can feel the distortion in the flow of life force. That is the aim: to feel their distortion and work to process it.

The reason the trauma doesn't get out of control and become overwhelming is because the patient doesn't let it. They have learnt how to suppress their trauma and they are good at dealing with it, *in small doses*. The therapist can feel how much effort the patient is using to suppress the issue and they say 'off' before it becomes too much and gets out of control.

So we have isolated a small piece of their distortion and need to get them to process it. Processing will happen automatically just by holding it in place by keeping them focussed and stopping them from getting distracted. That is what traumas do given the space, time and lack of overwhelm. The distortion goes through a series of contortions but, eventually, the distortion returns to a still point. Returning to a still point always happens and can take anything from a few seconds to a couple of minutes. When that has occurred the small piece of the trauma has been processed. The process of 'ticket on', gather a small piece of trauma, 'ticket off', process to a still point is repeated. It is repeated because every trauma is made up of small, manageable pieces. And because of this, every trauma can be transformed.

We repeat the process until when they connect with the trauma there is only peace and they are in a still point. They can think about the trauma without having to distract themselves and the dance is complete.

Trauma truths

Sometimes, it feels like the traumatised person doesn't want to remove their trauma and they may give many reasons why they don't want to. All of these reasons appear valid to the person but none of them are real. They are the reasons the person is maintaining their trauma and they do this because they don't want to be hurt. They know they have to process the trauma to be rid of it but they take the short-term view that processing it is harder than living with it. This is rarely the case. The feeling usually comes from failed attempts at processing it by themselves or with a clumsy therapist. The solution is to go slowly and take very small pieces to process each cycle until they get confidence in the technique.

When an incident is cleared the trauma won't have a disordered flow of life force attached to it and any symptom associated with the trauma will disappear. The only exceptions are when the symptoms have left a physical scar. All mental and emotional scars can be healed and every single perceived negative symptom can be turned into its positive equivalent. Lessons learnt are preserved but fears disappear.

In processing the trauma, it isn't the story of what happened that needs to be replayed. As I have said before, the story gets spoken about in counselling, psychotherapy and possibly with friends but, as a method of clearing, talking about the trauma is inefficient and often takes years and many unnecessary tears. Replaying the story of the incident isn't the solution because the incident *isn't stored as a story*. Instead, the incident is stored as a distortion in the flow of life force. Without understanding the flow of life force anyone administering to a trauma victim will be clumsy and probably inefficient.

This distortion in the flow of life force can be felt by a trained person who can guide the person to clear the trauma. The trained person and the patient don't get stuck in the story. All the person has to do is connect with the story in their head. The story in their head isn't the same as the story they would relate. The story in their head may be chronologically out of order, indeed time may do a lot of weird things in the story. The story may contain inexplicable feelings, it may even be distorted in terms of place but all of this doesn't matter. There will be one efficient path through the mess; that path belongs to the patient alone and that is what needs to be followed and processed. Deviations from this path are sometimes necessary to clear up a misconception or an incorrect assumption but having done that a return to the patient's path is the most efficient next step.

Contrary to what many people say and experience, resolving trauma, stress and panic attacks is easy. Indeed, when people experience the technique they often think they have cheated because so little effort was needed. Belief in the life force is not necessary. Using the life force is like not understanding what imaginary numbers or complex numbers are but still using them and getting solutions that you wouldn't have done without using them. (I am sorry if the analogy confused you but I used to be a mathematics teacher. The point is using the life force might not be scientific but it yields results that aren't available if you don't use it.)

How we can become resilient to trauma

Trauma can occur in anyone. All you need is for the information coming in to be greater than can be processed. But as people age and experience more life events, each life event that is experienced and processed enables them to cope with more and more potentially traumatising events. In this way, as people experience more they become more resilient.

We train children this way. People often have pets and it might be devastating when a pet dies but usually the event is processed reasonably quickly without much help, especially if the pet has a naturally short lifespan. The next time a pet dies it has already become a bit more commonplace. These deaths don't harden a person, instead the person gets to know how to process death so that when a grandparent dies, although it might be a difficult event, it doesn't have to turn into a traumatic one.

Compare this with someone who has never experienced death; the shock of the grandparent dying could be exceedingly traumatic. Indeed, if it is mishandled, even the shock of a goldfish dying could be traumatic. Everyone's situation is different.

Of course, if the death of the original pet wasn't dealt with properly and taken to peace but instead brushed under the carpet, when the second pet dies the trauma of the first unresolved pet's death will rear its head and double the intensity of the event. Time to get a bigger carpet. In this case, when the grandparent's time comes to an end, the death could be a traumatic incident. Having pets isn't the solution to teaching children about death, although it might help if managed well. The solution is taking events to peace and a still point.

When someone knows that it is possible to take any of their problems to a still point they gain in confidence. It is a marvellous thing to see and they become resilient to new traumas.

From my clinical experience, 75% of traumas that come to my clinic can be dealt with in less than a day. 15% may take one extra day. The remaining 10% need a different sort of approach. This may happen because the person concerned holds a view which stops them moving forward or they keep the trauma in place because of a circular argument or the patient believes that being seen as traumatised is of some benefit. These ideas need a logical breakdown in collaboration with an experienced person. It is extremely rare that traumas cannot be taken to peace, quickly and easily.

Traumas don't need to be that large to create physical sensations. Often traumas are caused because parents, and people in authority, don't know what they are doing.

How we keep traumas in place and fail to deal with them

The mind follows pathways already set up. Sometimes it uses paths that were set up for other reasons and they are often the ones that cause a conflict. For example, if you tended to avoid issues when you were young, you are more likely to do so when you are older. If you got away with lying to avoid difficulties, that behaviour may continue.

Being aggressive is another strategy that can work for a short time. Other ways of not dealing with a trauma are: ignoring problems; displacement activity; discharging emotionally out of context; avoidance through using alcohol; not eating; overeating; and worrying.

When any trauma is fully taken to peace that trauma is 100% dealt with and can't return without us making an effort to bring it back.

Contrary to popular belief you don't need to talk about your feelings to deal with your feelings.

Panic attacks

What is the purpose of a panic attack? All panic attacks have a purpose. But because therapists don't understand the role of the life force and I-force they believe panic attacks can come along for no reason. This is absolute twaddle. A panic attack is your mind's attempt to remove an unresolved emotional difficulty by replaying it while you are in a safe place. It might not be a safe place as far as you are concerned but it will be as far as your mind is concerned. The unresolved emotional difficulty that has caused the panic attack, might not be immediately obvious but it is definitely there and your mind definitely wants it to be resolved.

When confronted by a panic attack most people want to curtail it, by any means possible, but this stops it from resolving and keeps it in place. Rather than curtailing it, if we could slow it down so that we could handle the feelings that come with it, it could get resolved and completed.

Panic attacks occur because the mind tries to remove the unresolved problem by re-living it and this shows the power of the I-force. It is the I-force that can produce elevated heart rate, sweating, pains in the chest and all the other symptoms associated with panic attacks.

When you experience anything over and over again it becomes boring and starts to 'disappear'. Your mind knows this and will attempt to employ this tactic for any experience you have that is left unresolved. This repetition naturally comes to an end if allowed to complete. Each time your mind loops the unresolved event, if it is allowed to complete, it gets quicker and requires less effort, until it also becomes boring. If not allowed to complete, as in the case of an interrupted panic attack, it stays as a problem and, because of the fear of the ego, can even become a bigger problem.

Examples of events that can 'disappear' are the ticking of a clock. The ticking doesn't get quieter but over time its ticking appears to get quieter. The rising of the sun is an amazing event but is so often just taken for granted, having lost its awe. It loses its power through repetition. A light coming on when you flick a switch is a miracle of science but has happened to us so often it is only considered exciting if the light fails to come on. Even though the 'event of the ticking clock' has been processed and you don't hear the ticking you can still direct your mind to hear it, if necessary. The same is true for resolved trauma, it becomes boring. When properly resolved you can still recall the event but the difference now is that there is a 'pathway' through the event that brings you out the other side, to peace and a still point.

A patient of mine used to have panic attacks when she started to travel on a motorway. She was alone in her car, travelling along in a comfortable way, quite content. She might be unique, in that her mind thought this was an ideal time to sort out the trauma she had squirrelled away. My patient thought she had a problem with motorways but her problems disappeared as soon as we cleared her unresolved traumas.

Trying to stop trauma with medication or using techniques to avoid the issue will not succeed and will probably keep it in place, especially if initially there is minor improvement. The minor improvement gives you hope. The ONLY way to get rid of it is to play it out, to process it. Drugs keep the trauma in place. Counselling and therapy play it out with words but words unnecessarily prolong the agony. The quickest most efficient way is to play it out is done using the Boulderstone Technique.

In resolving panic attacks with the Boulderstone Technique, no force is required. Very little trauma is experienced. It is much easier than talking about the problem. Working through the problem with the Boulderstone Technique is rapid, gentle and permanent. (See Appendix)

Anger (and happiness and sadness)

If you have ever really analysed any anger you have around a person you will find that you aren't really angry with them. This goes for everyone, every time. This is a marvellous truth that actually allows everyone to heal from the worst crimes that could ever be inflicted. You are NEVER angry for the reason you think you are. Generally, most people have got anger wrong.

If you analyse the anger you hold toward a person you will see that they couldn't help what they did or it wasn't their fault or they were only a pawn in the game. But you might have blamed them for a long time. Why do we do this? Could it be that by externalising our anger we protect our ego? Underlying anger there is often a layer of fear.

If you accept the phrase 'You are never angry for the reason you think you are' as true, are there any other phrases like that, that we also get wrong? Such as, 'You are never happy for the reason you think you are' and 'You are never sad for the reason you think you are'.

The key point is anger, happiness and sadness aren't feelings that come from the outside but are generated within us. They all come from a distortion in the flow of *our* life force. We are angry, happy or sad depending on what we feel within us and we have control over that. External reasons for those three feelings aren't accurate. If they were then those events would make everyone happy, sad or angry, equally. Clearly, anger, happiness and sadness are caused by something resonating within each of us. It isn't the external events that change our feelings but how we respond to those events.

Our feelings are under our control. The feelings you hold about a murderer who has killed one of your children is generated by you not the murderer or the murder. Directing those feelings outward toward the perpetrator may make you temporarily feel better but that won't stop the feelings. The feelings also won't be stopped by the apprehension and conviction of the killer. Feelings only come from the person experiencing them, they aren't caused by outside events.

One of the experiences that led me to this conclusion was a press conference of a mother forgiving the murderer of her child even before he had been caught. Initially, I couldn't understand it. Didn't she love her daughter? But she understood that harbouring strong feelings towards her child's murderer was only going to damage her and do nothing to the killer.

If you have anger inside you that you believe is caused by someone else's actions, it can give you a strong motivating force to 'right the wrong'. For this reason, it could give you purpose and could be seen as desirable. The problem is one doesn't usually need motivation to 'right a wrong'. Externalising a motivating force takes responsibility away from you and you might find that useful but it comes at a price. That price is burnout, despair and frustration as you work at something your 'heart' isn't fully behind even if your ego is. Having a bunch of bad mathematics teachers gave me the energy to get a maths degree and a teaching certificate. I spent years slowly realising being a maths teacher was not what I wanted to do. Externalising a motivating force doesn't last forever.

ALL feelings you have get transformed when they are processed. If your starting point is anger at someone, as you examine why you are angry you will eventually realise you are really angry at something you did or didn't do. It always comes back to you. When you process the anger it transforms into a still point and disappears, always.

It is possible to process other feelings as well. What if you process happiness? Surely, that is a feeling that doesn't need processing? It does. Like anger, it is a feeling that has been created by your ego and is temporary and when it is absent you might say you are sad. Both sadness and happiness can be processed. When you process happiness it ends in joy. Joy is intimately connected with happiness, it just has the ego aspect of it removed. Joy is a universal feeling whereas happiness is personal. Sadness processed ends in a still point and peace. So the question becomes 'How do you feel peace?' That is the biggest question.

There are many feelings that, as human beings, we dislike, such as inadequacy, depression, frustration, anxiety and grief. They are all based in our ego and, as such, can be processed into peace. This is because peace is our natural state. Our ego is what has made us the dominant species on the planet but it is also our Achilles' heel, unless we truly understand it's purpose.

Anxiety

Anxiety is a symptom. It is the mind's solution to a problem, the problem being 'Should I do this' or 'Should I do that'. So what is the problem? If your *feelings* conflict with what you know, what do you do? Of course, different people do different things but, when there is that conflict, some people will follow their heart and some their head.

Others won't be sure and oscillate between their thoughts and their feelings. It is at this point that the person will experience indecision. And when this indecision is speeded up, by the mind in an attempt to get to a solution, anxiety will result. It is important to realise the cause is the difficulty trusting wholeheartedly in either the thoughts or feelings and the anxiety stems from that indecision. In other words, it is a symptom. Treating the symptom without looking at the cause will always make the person worse off. And worse off could mean being addicted to the bogus solution.

The real solution is understanding how the mind works.

When a person is flip-flopping between thoughts and feelings, a Boulderstone Technique practitioner with hands on the patient's head can feel this taking place. The thing about every human being is that, in every situation, they will tend to decide what path to take with either their thoughts or feelings. The practitioner has nothing to do with this decision; the patient does that for themselves given the space and time.

All the practitioner needs to do is allow the flip-flopping to continue until it stops and it does always stop. As long as focus is maintained and no distractions occur, it will compete. The flip-flopping can be tedious and tiring; after all who wants to be doing that all day? Left to their own devices the patient doesn't let it finish naturally, instead they usually stop the process before it resolves by modifying their thinking in some way. They interrupt the process by watching television, having a cup of tea or coffee or a cigarette or exercising. Anything to stop the chatter in their mind, but what this change of topic does is keep the anxiety in place by not completing it.

I regularly see people who have something they have been anxious about for a long time that gets cleared in less than 10 minutes, by following this process and all without talking about the issue because the mental/emotional anxiety is felt physically by the practitioner and resolved or processed.

Like all the other feelings, anxiety only exists in the anxious person's mind.

Grief

Grief is a natural reaction to a loss but what naturally happens is you work through it. For some people this can take a short time and for others it appears to go on forever. This is where your flow of life force is hindered by your thoughts or beliefs, your I-force, which can often get in the way. Each time you work through your particular stumbling blocks they get easier. By the time you have worked through them a hundred, or a thousand or a million times it gets quicker and easier because you aren't fighting the flow of life force as much. You are accepting the situation. Eventually, there is no restriction to the flow of life force and you work through the issues almost instantaneously. That is the end of the grief.

So what are the barriers we put up, in grief, to distort the flow of life force and slow down the process? Fixed beliefs are one of the biggest. One of the first questions I ask patients in grief is, 'What do you believe happens after you die?' Now, I would like to point out that my belief is irrelevant. But from experience, I have found that people who believe 'nothing happens' take much longer to get over their grief. Indeed, if it is a strong feeling of 'nothing happens' then they might not ever get over it.

Of the two forces we each have, the life force and the I-force, each has a different 'view' of death. The life force is forever free and sees death as a part of life. The I-force on the other hand is much more fixed and sees death as the absolute end. Anyone who believes that 'nothing happens' after death lives centred in the I-force. Having this belief is enough to stop grief getting processed.

To counter this problem I point out that nobody knows what happens after death and it is possible that something does happen. All I ask is that the person concerned is open to the possibility that something could happen after death, we just don't know. That openness (to a little life force) is enough to get through that first sticking point of grief.

If the person is still in grief then they aren't at a still point and are getting stuck somewhere else. If this is the case then the grief will be felt as a physical tension and removing that tension is done in the same way as described in 'Processing an event or trauma', earlier in the chapter.

Obsessions

One of the many unique things about the Boulderstone Technique is that it doesn't need an external classification system to describe an illness. No diagnosis is needed or even wanted. We don't need to diagnose an illness because that is already done when the patient says 'something isn't right'. The patient always knows when something isn't right although they don't always know when something isn't wrong! If a person 'makes up' being ill then there is certainly something that needs to be addressed. Illness has been complicated by Western medicine because of its need for objective, measurable symptoms and inability to define health positively.

An obsession is a distortion in the flow of life force that causes a person to repeat a pattern of behaviour. The behaviour may appear to be beneficial or it may be detrimental but either way it is an illness. A distortion in the flow of life force is always a negative thing, even when it leads to a positive habit, as it keeps one away from the still point. Waking every morning and exercising may appear to be a good habit but when it is driven by a distortion in the flow of life force it is an obsession, keeps you away from peace and will eventually produce symptoms.

How to cause an obsession

If you have an obsession it was caused by an experience that has not been processed. This means that any time your mind thinks you are in the right space, it looks for a way to get you to re-live the experience. Your ego then looks around for a way to escape re-living the experience, and discovers an activity that seems to do the job. If the escape activity works in different situations it won't take long before it becomes an obsession.

Obsession-causing experiences are usually sexual abuse, near-death experiences, violence or even experiencing a family dynamic without appropriate context or maturity. Of course there are others but these are most common. These are not trivial experiences and sensitive people will be more susceptible, due to having a lower pain threshold. If your mind manages to find an escape in the form of an easy to repeat activity, an obsession could be born.

The escape could be anything but the main problems we get asked to deal with seem to be: repeatedly checking locks or gas/electrical appliances, 'difficult' thoughts resulting in distracting behaviours and fears around health often resulting in obsessive washing or cleaning. Those activities appear to be important enough to engulf the person in the activity so they can escape the processing of the difficult experience.

In many cases, the person believes the activity is important so that if it is not completed something significantly awful could happen and they would be responsible. The thinking would be something like: 'If I complete the activity I can escape having to deal with the original experience, and if I don't complete the activity I could be responsible for a catastrophe.' Once the activity is completed they are back needing an escape again and in their loop: complete the activity or be responsible for a catastrophe.

It should be clear that the escape activity, which has turned into an obsession, is not the real problem. Forcing the cessation of the escape activity does not solve the problem. Yet that, it appears, is what most people try to do with Anorexia or Tourettes or other Obsessive-Compulsive Disorders.

Unfortunately, sometimes the original experience that caused the obsession can get lost. One reason this can happen, is that the original problem was not fully understood and so there is no way to explain it or retain it as a logical memory. An example being when children hear or see something of an adult nature. Another reason could be when children get sent off to boarding school or lose a parent. In these cases the problem only exists as a feeling and a counsellor will only ever help with the symptoms always leaving the cause in place which inevitably will create a bigger problem.

Traditional Anorexia Nervosa treatment seems to be centred around a symptom, namely how much the person is eating as measured by their weight. I have emphasised in this book that the symptom is not the problem and working with it and changing it is always going to be detrimental to the patient. I realise that what I am saying is that if a person with Anorexia puts on weight that is a bad thing but I stand by what I have said. If the cause of the illness is not addressed, removing symptoms makes the person worse. Of course, when someone's life is threatened that has to be the highest priority before dealing with any cause.

The solution to all these problems comes about when we make the distinction between physical and emotional pain. Acute physical pain is there to tell us to avoid something, to not do that again, such as when you put your hand in a fire. Your body gives you acute pain to tell you to not do that again. Acute physical pain is saying 'run away'. Emotional pain is saying the opposite. It is saying, 'Follow this pain to a still point.' Or go into it and explore it. Understanding there is a huge difference between physical and emotional pain is the key to unlocking obsessions and compulsions. It is unfortunate that the word pain is used in both instances.

The trauma that the mind is avoiding isn't always obvious. It may have happened before it was possible to understand the situation as in the case of a baby being operated on without anaesthetic in the belief it would forget the experience. Or it could happen that they were sexually assaulted at five years old. Or it could be any other experience that wasn't understood at the time.

The mind stores memories (the dance) in images, feelings and thoughts but not usually in words. Using words to try and sort them out is, at best, going to be extremely laboured if not impossible. How do you describe your 'dance' with words? Each 'dance' has so many nuances, so many turns, feelings, smells, thoughts, sensations, tastes and images that words will never do it justice, not for me at any rate.

So, with compulsive activity, the mind might always be on alert, looking out for traumas so that it can avoid them. To process a trauma the mind needs to re-live the situation and simultaneously view it objectively. If the mind can stay in its still point when viewing the trauma, the trauma will be permanently removed. That's great, except the still point is inaccessible because to get there the mind needs to have every trauma cleared. In this case the mind has to be creative to stop reliving the trauma so it creates another dance, the escape activity.

The compulsive person needs to understand a red flag thrown up by their mind getting close to finding a trauma is not something to be feared. But this behaviour is learnt before they found another way and it works. The problem comes when the escape activity is destructive.

Example

My only compulsive behaviour existed when I was in my twenties and I still find it embarrassing. It started when I started driving. I was an inexperienced driver and the first time I drove a car on my own I narrowly missed having a head-on collision with another car. I was petrified but I held my breath and stuffed the feelings back down. I had found my escape activity. Every time from then on whenever I went under a bridge I had to hold my breath. I felt if I didn't hold my breath I would die. Every time I didn't quite make it because the tunnel was too long I thought I would die. It took me years to leave this compulsion behind but I know I got rid of it by processing the fear that resulted from that near head-on accident. Forcing myself to take breaths in a tunnel or under a bridge, dealing with the symptom, hadn't worked after ten years.

Having a Boulderstone Technique practitioner feel your tension and understand what is happening when you confront or get close to the trauma that started your compulsion, work through it and get to a still point without triggering the escape activity will remove any compulsion.

The obsession is not the problem. It is trying to save you from harm, serious illness or death by filling your consciousness with something that will take over those thoughts. There is always a solution and that solution will involve moving to a still point.

Spider phobia

Seeing how a person is after removing a spider phobia compared to the way they were before, you can tell that the spider, as an object, has very little to do with problem. When the phobia has gone the person can be fascinated by spiders: the way they move; how they look; what they eat and every other aspect of the arachnid's life. The symptom is not the problem. So what is?

I would like to point out that current treatments for spider phobia are not efficient. Basically they aim to change the way you think about spiders. They do this by creeping up on the feeling and modifying how you react to that particular feeling as in Cognitive Behavioural Therapy (CBT) and hypnosis. Or exposure therapy, where the patient is gradually exposed to pictures of spiders and slowly moving on the real thing. All these therapies deal with the symptoms not the cause.

The way I deal with a person who has a spider phobia (and any other phobia) is the same way I deal with stress. I ask the question: 'How do you know you have a problem with spiders? What in you mind or body is telling you that this is a problem?'

The answer always comes down to the same thing: there is a physical tension located somewhere in the body (a different place for different people). That is how people recognise there is danger and it seems to arrive before the interpretation of the physical feeling, namely fear.

Now is that the real cause? No it is not but it is closer to the cause than cognitive symptoms and, crucially, that tension can be felt by another person. Using the same method of removing the stress described in the section: Chapter 7: Processing an event or trauma, removes the physical sensation and consequently the fear. And once removed the patient is free to love spiders.

The problem doesn't come back.

This solution usually takes one session: no mind games, no trickery, a genuinely beautiful solution.

See what a patient said about her spider phobia session. *'I was absolutely terrified of spiders. I couldn't ever rest and I was constantly tense in case there was a spider in the room. I would scream and climb on the table if one came into the room. I was petrified one might climb up my leg. After only 3 sessions of the Boulderstone Technique I am* **no longer frightened of spiders at all***. I touched a spider on the fence outside - a big black wood spider. Today I held a tarantula in my hand. It was lovely, soft, furry and tickly. I'm thinking of getting one as a pet. I can't believe it - the fear has completely gone!*

Phobias are easy to deal with but only if you use the life force.

Depression

The first thing to say is that depression is a symptom not a cause. Prescribing anti-depressants for depression might make the depression feel different but it does nothing for the real illness. It might feel that depression can come about for no reason but that is never the case. Instead, there is always a distortion in the flow of life force from an inner battle. But if the inner battle isn't easily discerned then then it could be that it has come about unconsciously. Our minds are incredibly clever and can work out a lot without any conscious input. You can often see this when you wake in the morning with a new idea or solution to a problem you went to sleep with. You have been unconsciously, in sleep, working out a logical extension of your current thoughts. This nocturnal thinking can go on independently of your conscious thoughts but can also work against you.

Depression can be understood by first looking at the opposite. The opposite of depression is a wide-eyed wonder that is most often seen in children seeing something for the first time. Like the first time they see a rainbow or experience thunder and lightning or a circus or snow. It is one reason we take children to events such as these to 'be infected by' their enthusiasm and give them a sense of awe at the infinite. All of those experiences, seen through the eyes of a child, have the effect they do because, to the watcher they are overwhelming without being (too) frightening. As far as the child is concerned there is an aspect of infinity at play.

When you are depressed you look at the world without the wide-eyed wonder. Your world has shrunk for you, instead of being infinite it has become smaller.

Your world can shrink for many reasons, it can happen slowly and it can even happen overnight without much conscious thinking on your part. However, the shrinking only occurs if you have a fixed belief about the way things are. For example, say you have a categorical belief that after you die absolutely nothing happens. Eventually, and possibly in your sleep, your brain works out that you are alive for a finite amount of time and then you die and nothing happens and, therefore, nothing really matters. Your world has shrunk. Clearly, the cause, in this example, is the belief that nothing happens after you die. The result of this belief could be the *symptom* of depression, pointing you to the problem. Treating the symptom with antidepressants is absurd in that cure can never be the result.

Or it could be that you have a categorical belief that after you die you go on to an afterlife. In that case you might believe that it doesn't matter whether you live or die in this life because there is always the next one. If you perceive your current life as lacking in some way you could get the symptom of depression but it would be pointing to your belief about what happens after you die.

Symptoms are the warning signs that something is wrong, that there is a mistake in your thinking. Symptoms are always trying to help you but it is important to read them the right way. The cause of depression will always come down to a belief that the world is a particular way and that way is a choice. This does not mean that a depressed person is wilfully causing their depression, they are always doing the best they can but sometimes their beliefs clash.

The solution to these problems is to process the incorrect belief by feeling what it does and allowing it to complete its job. The symptom, feeling of depression, can be used as a *starting point*, it will created by a physical feeling somewhere in the body. The physical feeling tells the person they are depressed and is caused by some beliefs, clashing. This is the real problem. Resolution of this physical feeling will clear the depression.

Getting put on antidepressants by a doctor after hearing

how your world has shrunk is bordering on criminal. Of course, few people can do anything about the real world events but that doesn't mean depression is inevitable.

Whenever you can't do something you want to there is inner contradiction. When it happens in children, it can result in a temper tantrum. When the same thing happens in an adult they tend to bury the problem. This burying is an inner contradiction and will result in symptoms. In my experience if the inner contradiction is mild something like a cold results. If the conflict is bigger something like flu results and if the conflict is even bigger something like anxiety or depression results. I don't deny the existence of bacteria or viruses but the conflict always come first.

Multiple Sclerosis (MS)

MS is another example of Western medicine describing a condition and calling it a disease. Sclerosis, in this context, means scarring of the myelin sheath surrounding the nerve cell causing the nerve to not work well. I am not a doctor but that doesn't stop me from speaking to people and, through doing that, I have found the one thing that is common to all of my hundreds of patients who have been diagnosed with MS.

MS comes about because the person made a decision that seemed like a good one at the time but long term it turned out to be a disaster. That decision was to not process an emotional event and instead suppress or avoid it.

To illustrate this, I am going to relate three cases of people who have been diagnosed with MS. They are horrible stories and I hope you never get put in their positions but, if you are, just know that it is always possible to find a way to be free of your problems, healthy and happy.

The Western Medical model of MS is that it comes from out of the blue, attacks for no reason and it can get you at any time. This description is absurd. There is always a build-up to MS, it does not come about for no reason. The symptoms of the disease are that certain nerves get inflamed and then lose their protective outer coating which may cause pain and those nerves eventually stop working. But inflammation is the physical body's attempt to sort things out; it must have detected a problem. Pain is a symptom telling your mind to 'look here'. Of course, people try and ignore the symptoms by taking painkillers, anti-inflammatories and steroids. Painkillers, anti-inflammatories and steroids are the sticking plasters placed over the warning lights of the body and Western medicine's medication of choice.

We are told regularly, in the media, that medication for the disease will be available in the next fifty years, so all you have to do is wait. Nothing could be further from the truth. The idea that MS just comes from out of the blue for no reason is frankly not credible. Not a single thing in the world happens for no reason, not one. So to state that diseases are the only thing to have no cause is someone trying to pull the wool over your eyes. But the idea that the disease is caused by the patient is also frightening. Frightening for the patient and frightening for their physician. People with MS have their physical body slowly taken away from them and to believe they consciously do this to themselves is also clearly absurd. There will never be a pharmaceutical cure in fifty years or even five hundred years because the disease is not based on the destruction of the nerve covering. That is a symptom.

When I put my hands on a patient diagnosed with MS, I can feel a tension in their body that is sufficient to cause the nerves passing through that tension to stop working. That tension might have been there for twenty, thirty, forty or more years and it is there because of the patient's story, their dance. And in that story, they chose to suppress what they were feeling because they didn't know another way of dealing with their pain. The seeds for MS are often sown in childhood. If a child experiences severe trauma, such as the loss of a parent, they deal with it as best they can at the time, in order to survive. They are often not guided to process their trauma in the best possible way, but instead they clamp down on their emotions and bury them deep. They have learnt how not to process trauma but to hold on to it and tense up around it. When stressful events happen throughout their life they are likely to use the same survival method, accumulating more and more unprocessed trauma until they start to have physical problems. They have become so tense that they are crushing their nerves in a similar way to when you get 'pins and needles'.

Let's take a look at a few real examples.

Case 1:

Killing a person isn't an easy thing to do but it happens that some people legally kill others. Killing someone while defending your country is considered just by most people. For the person concerned it might not feel that way, though.

While on patrol in Northern Ireland during 'the troubles' a soldier's platoon came under attack The soldier swung round, saw a person standing in a window with a rifle, shot and killed him. The whole incident took only a few seconds and he might never have been able to replicate that shot. The soldier had not been mentally prepared for what had happened, though, and could not come to terms with taking a life. Even though he was a trained soldier and it was his job and he was protecting his platoon. He kept his thoughts to himself and whenever the memory of the incident was stimulated he would tense his body and the thought that he had done something wrong would be frozen.

He became skilled at not thinking about the incident through tensing. He knew he was in the 'right', everyone told him he was. He wasn't happy for the dead person's family but that wasn't his responsibility. The trouble was he identified with the person he had killed. He was about the same age and had children the same age as his own but it didn't matter because he was in the 'right'. And while he could tense himself he could stop any feelings from surfacing. He was diagnosed with MS two years after the incident and discharged from the army.

Unbelievably, at least to me, his doctors said there was no connection between the killing and the MS but I am pretty sure if he had not killed that person he wouldn't have MS.

Case 2:

Killing your own child isn't unheard of. The statistics say that the majority of perpetrators have mental problems but a smaller number believe they are doing something 'right'. If it can be seen that the child is going to suffer for its whole life, many parents would consider death to be an option. The problem is, you can never tell anyone if you decide to do it. I heard of a single mother who was put in this position and she decided to kill her child as she believed it was the 'right' thing to do. It doesn't matter whether you agree with her or not. Some people and the law would probably say it was wrong but that thought was suppressed by the patient by creating what I have come to see as the MS tension. Just six months after her child died she was diagnosed with MS. No connection was made by doctors, she was just considered unlucky.

Case 3:

A young girl wanted a pony and pestered her mother for one. The mother wasn't a particularly kind person but on this occasion decided, for her own reasons, to acquiesce. They went together to purchase the pony and while they were buying it the daughter heard someone say something strange. What she heard was to change her life. She heard a person say that anyone buying that pony was trying to kill the person who would ride it because it was so difficult to ride. The child didn't say a word because she believed her mother was trying to kill her. She kept the thought buried for twenty-five years and she buried it by creating the 'MS tension'. All that time she believed her mother was trying to kill her and there was no one she could talk to about it. She was diagnosed with MS in her late thirties. Was her mother really trying to kill her? I doubt it but that thought caused sufficient tension in her head to cause inflammation of the nerves and a deterioration of the myelin sheath. When she learnt to let go of the tension her MS stopped getting worse.

MS and Stress

In every case of MS there is a huge tension when the person connects with their 'issue', the MS-tension. Patients often have a stiff neck (75% plus) and will often choose the right thing to do but in their heart, they know it is suspect. In my opinion, every single case of MS yields to *connecting the issue to the still point*.

MS relapses *always* come about through stress. This is often ignored by doctors who don't know how to measure stress or even what to do with it. Stress is *always* caused by the person experiencing the stress. I am not saying that an MS relapse is consciously caused by the patient but it can be consciously removed by the patient.

In MS, cannabis is often self-prescribed as it relaxes the MS-tension but, like all medications, it does not and cannot cure. Clearing out the MS-tension can be achieved with the Boulderstone Technique but the damage caused by the scarring can't be undone by the therapy.

I hope I have made it clear that the judgement of another person in doing what they do does not help me and it does not help them. Everyone does whatever they do because they think it is the best thing they can do. That goes for every person in every situation. They are not always right though.

Cancer

Cancer, like MS and everything else in this world, doesn't come from nowhere. Nothing comes from nowhere; everything has a cause. Doctors often say that cancer can just come from out of the blue, for no reason, but they are wrong. Nothing happens for no reason. Perhaps they don't look for the cause because they are only interested in symptoms.

There are cancers that appear to result from obvious external factors, such as sun radiation, tobacco, asbestos and other inappropriate ingested substances (but they really come about through our internal reaction to those substances). They have come about because the body has been overwhelmed by a difficult substance which has distorted the way our body grows. Everybody grows and everybody is growing, all the time. It doesn't matter if you are eight minutes old or eighty years old, if you are alive, you are growing. Our continual growth is what accounts for the fact that we heal, learn, feel new things, live and love. It is often said that you stop growing after the age of sixteen or eighteen or some other arbitrary age but while it might be true for our height, it is simply not true for the whole body. Our hair grows and so do our nails; our skin gets replaced; our bones regrow when broken; our organs heal. Growth goes on all the time. The question is how do all those growing parts know how to grow correctly and what happens if that growing information gets distorted?

Before I talk about distorted growing information I need to talk about the UK 1939 Cancer Act. The 1939 Cancer Act was brought in to stop quacks from making money by claiming they had found a cure. I understand the need for this and I wouldn't prevent anyone who wanted to from seeing a doctor. I can't and don't diagnose cancer or the absence of it, I don't give medicines for cancer, I certainly don't perform surgery and I don't suggest to clients they don't need to see a doctor and I will continue not to treat cancer. But I do treat *people* and sometimes those people have been diagnosed with cancer.

You always get an indication, sometimes years in advance, that something isn't right and there is a distortion in the flow of life force and you avoid this feeling at your own expense. However, the body always grows according to the flow of life force and if that flow is disordered then so will be anything that grows from that place. An indication that something is wrong might be a tickle or an itch that goes on for months, or a pain that goes on for months, or something else that just doesn't seem right and goes on for much longer than it should.

The body grows according to the flow of life force. If the flow of life force is distorted, the body will grow in a distorted way (see arthritis in Chapter 9). If the life force is forced to double back on itself and continues to double back on itself, a tumour could result.

For example: If you have a secret that you have never told anyone or that has never been processed, something

127

that you keep worrying about and you can feel in your body, it could cause a tumour. If that situation also makes you cringe when you think about it, it could cause a malignant tumour. This situation could arise because you did something that you know was dreadful and every time you think about it you feel sick to your stomach. (Examples could be: you put a banana skin where you knew someone would walk and they slipped and broke their arm; or you trod on and killed your pet hamster; or, as a nurse, you gave your patient the wrong medicine and they died.) And every time you have that feeling of anguish, you try to reverse it and double back on it rather than process it. In this situation you create, by your actions, a life force loop that will inevitably cause symptoms. If this goes on for several years the continual doubling back of your life force will create a doubling back of the way your physical body grows. (Remember the symptoms arise so that you can deal with the problem - how else do you think your body communicates with you?) Problems always arise if you don't deal with a situation. The natural growth and replenishment of cells grow according to the flow of life force. A life force that doubles back on itself will inevitably cause symptoms. Surgery, drugs and counselling will not change the problem.,

As an alternative health practitioner I don't treat any diseases, something doctors often find difficult to get their heads around. Instead, I work with people and the things they do that get in the way of them getting better. For example, a patient of mine came to see me after his child had died. The following year he was diagnosed with Multiple Sclerosis (apparently an incurable disease without a known cause - I am being sarcastic) and the rate at which he was having MS relapses meant he was heading for serious problems. His consultant told him the MS diagnosis had nothing to do with his son dying, and the patient wasn't sure what to believe. However, I could tell immediately that many of his problems arose from the way he was dealing with his grief. The point was he wasn't dealing with it at all. Instead he was using force to stop himself thinking about it. This was getting in the way of his health. After using my technique for removing unwanted and difficult emotional problems his MS symptoms went away and even five years later he doesn't have MS relapses at all. I didn't treat the MS, instead I 'treated' his inability to deal with grief. Perhaps it was a co-incidence that his MS got better. Personally I don't think it was but how can we ever know?

The point is that people unwittingly put up obstacles to their natural healing which, if removed, could go a long way to sorting out their problems. I believe that unresolved emotional problems can cause growing information to get distorted. Clearing people's unresolved emotional problems may help with all sorts of illnesses; it isn't specifically aimed at cancer or MS or any other disease. Resolving emotional problems has many good side effects. What I know is that unresolved emotional problems distort growing information. You may ask how I know this. The answer is I can feel it. I feel it with my hands and my body.

For example, have you ever watched an upset person work through a problem and come out the other side without you getting in their way? If you are a parent it would be difficult to avoid. Did you notice how you lived the problem with the child but, probably because you have more life experience, you didn't get as upset as your child or the other person? When the person doesn't come out the other side they are left with an unresolved emotional problem. You can feel it. You can see it in virtually everything that person does. The closer you get to the person the more strongly you can feel it. If you put your hands on the person you feel it even more strongly. The question is: 'How much does the unresolved emotional problem affect that person and their health?' Could it be responsible for a cold? Could it be responsible for flu? I think bugs and viruses cause colds and flu but the susceptibility to colds and flu could certainly come from the effort of having to deal with an unresolved emotional problem.

What I also know is that there is a way to clear those unresolved emotional problems without having to talk about them. (Talking is the traditional way of dealing with them.) If you hold someone's head and feel an unresolved emotional problem in the person, and you can feel that problem in yourself and know how to deal with it, that information can be transferred to the other person in a matter of moments. That is what happened with the patient whose child had died. And that is what has happened with the thousands of patients I have worked with over the last thirty or so years.

Is this treatment? It isn't a traditional doctor-patient relationship, it is more akin to an education but it isn't teaching in a traditional manner either. As I have said I don't give medicines, I don't treat diseases, but I do 'treat' people with their unresolved emotional issues and many times when those problems have gone away so do their physical problems. A question you could ask yourself is 'Are my unresolved emotional problems sufficient to cause the problems I have?' If the answer is yes you might like to make an appointment.

So, what should you do if you have a symptom? You might feel nothing can be done about it and decide to just put up with it but that would be a mistake. Every symptom is your body trying to tell you something. You may be offered a steroid cream by a doctor but that is the equivalent of covering up a warning light because everything has a cause and it is important to find the cause. Covering up the warning is reasonable if the body can get on with doing the healing but without feedback the body could get confused. I would hazard a guess that covering up warning signs is the number one reason that people's health is deteriorating and is probably one of the reasons that cancer has increased in the last few decades. Symptoms are given more priority over causes to save time and effort.

Something is causing the increase in cancer and it isn't me or what I do. The fear, anxiety and trepidation caused by people being told that cancer comes from out of the blue, for no reason, borders on the criminal.

Autism

Autism has been in my family for generations. I suspect my grandfather was autistic. He killed himself after experiencing the horrors of war. My mother had autistic tendencies, as do I and also a brother. I have a daughter who is 'officially' diagnosed as are two grandchildren. All of us are intellectually sound, but have to find novel ways to deal with stimulation. As a result, I have some insight into the condition. Again, I want to repeat I am not a doctor and the views I put forward are my own opinions.

Our I-force contains the filters we 'see' through when we look at our life and any situation we find ourselves in. We use our ego and I-force to not look at, or only partially look at, the atrocities our governments perpetrate in our name. Or the injustices we see in the world. Too much contradiction and we lose energy, insight and objectivity.

The same is true for children: they have to block out the parts that they don't understand and use their ego and I-force to do it. But children are different because they have less experience and don't know which events are really serious and which are not. Consequently, everything has the potential to be overwhelming. What happens when they get overwhelmed? Normally they may have an outburst which might clear the problem and they would go back to clarity. But what would happen if they are very sensitive and they get overwhelmed? What would happen if they are very sensitive, they get overwhelmed and their pet dies? What would happen if they are very sensitive, they get overwhelmed, their pet dies and then they have a vaccination?

What do you do if you are completely overwhelmed and something else happens? Some scream, some cry, some break things, some get drunk and all the time what you are really doing is trying to get to a still point and peace. But what if you haven't been alive long enough to know that you always have a still point within you and it is only covered over with overwhelming thoughts? What if you think that entering a still point is like dying? After all it is a death for the ego but if you are young enough you might not have understood that the ego can die but always gets reborn, you still live. If it was a question of either your life or death and you could not communicate to anyone what you were going through, and you had to stimulate your senses in some way so that your ego could stay alive and you had to do that forever you might decide to withdraw, become obsessed with details, rock back and forth, stop talking, avoid eye contact and so on and develop autistic traits. It isn't that being sensitive is a problem or getting overwhelmed or losing a pet or getting multiple vaccinations but none of them help. They all cause stress and being able to cuddle up to a parent and slowly discharge might undo that stress unless touch has become an issue…

The vaccination schedule in the USA is incredibly large now, chiefly because the idea of avoiding obvious diseases is appealing. But only a few seconds of consideration is required to realise this isn't right. Our ancestors didn't get over twenty five vaccinations for over twelve diseases before the age of two. Many times the child will tell you vaccination cause stress by screaming and crying and what do the doctors and nurses do? They ignore it, talk over the screaming baby, make placating remarks that mean nothing. They have become hardened to the suffering of children. For what? Pharmaceutical companies lie, they say vaccines are safe and effective even though they don't definitively know that to be true. The physical stress of having such a huge amount of Aluminium, and other chemicals could easily be the straw that tips the child into permanent escape. The press seem to go along with the idea that they are safe and effective, also ignoring many studies about safe levels of chemicals. How long will it be before USA lapdogs follow suit and imposes a similar vaccine schedule.

As I have said many times, I am not a doctor but I have an ability that allows me to feel the distress in another human being. I call that distress a distortion in the flow of life force. If you could feel that distress (you can if you focus in the right area) you could feel the distress caused by a vaccination, you could feel the distress caused by the childhood illnesses and you would choose the illness over the vaccination every time.

I do not fully know whether the Boulderstone Technique can always help people diagnosed with autism but I do know it can help with anxiety, problems with being oversensitive, problems with grief and problems from vaccination. Changing the mind of a person with autism who believes that the only way to stay alive is to go down a path that creates weird symptoms requires them to trust me enough that they can suspend their belief that they are going to die and choose a different path. A big ask for anyone.

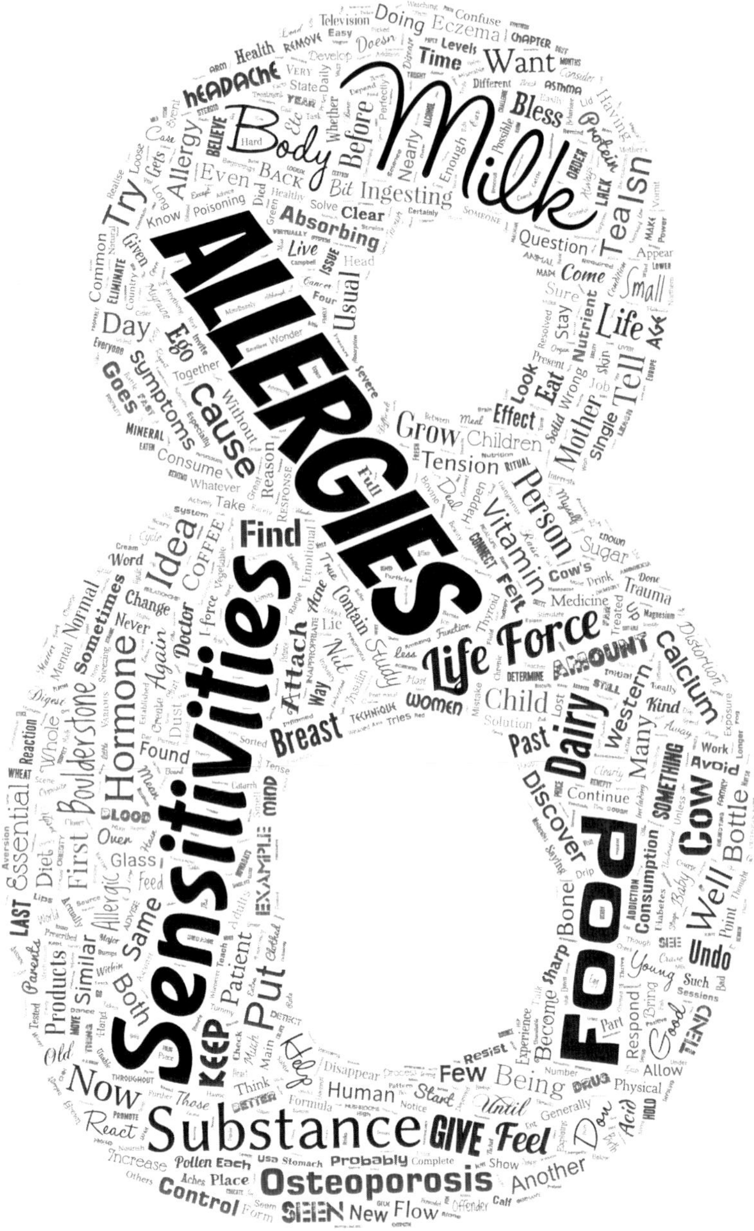

Chapter 8: Allergies and sensitivities

Beginnings

There were times when I wondered whether I was really feeling a distortion in the flow of life force because the movement was so subtle. But as time goes by, while I might still question myself over any number of things, those times have become much less frequent. Bringing something new into the world, like the Boulderstone Technique, has forced me to continually look at what I am doing, since there are very few people I can bounce ideas off. I still find it amazing that the people I have taught, and myself, appear to be the only ones using this technique to detect a person's sensitivity to substances, as well as undo traumas, both physical and mental. I think other people in the past probably did work in a similar way, with the life force, and this explains some behaviours that Western medicine now scorns. Saying grace before a meal might be one such ritual, or saying 'bless you' after sneezing. They are both examples of having some understanding of the life force.

Even coming from a mathematical and logical background, the very last thing I want to do is hurt someone by misinterpreting what I feel which is why I continually question what I am doing.

Nowadays, I realise that time has been a great teacher for me. I don't question myself nearly so much because feedback has been incredibly positive and people have reported that they have been helped. Human beings are sensitive and, if they can get their egos out of the way, they can feel the smallest of feelings in another person. Some people, especially mothers, can even feel things at a distance, in their children. They know what is happening but science doesn't back them up.

As I said, human beings are very sensitive and if you connect with them you can feel some of the things they feel. If you place some nuts on a person who is allergic to nuts their body goes tense and the person connected can feel that tension.

Early on I found it doesn't matter whether the substance was open or contained within a glass bottle with a screwed on lid. I don't want to talk about the limits of the sensitivity just yet because it is hard enough for me to believe. But that is how we discover if a person has a sensitivity to a food or other substance. We invite them to lie on a massage couch, place one hand under their head, and sequentially place small bottles of food and other substances on them and feel for a tension. With training you can detect the sensitivity in a person. Getting your ego out of the way is essential and is the main challenge.

All of this has little scientific underpinnings, as far as I know, except for one thing. If the person tested stops ingesting the substances that we find them sensitive to, they get better.

Many people are sensitive to cow's milk protein from birth. When the dairy is stopped they start to thrive and all their symptoms go away. When they start the dairy again, on the advice of doctors or because they want to believe they have grown out of it, either the old symptoms come back and/or new ones start up. For example, parents will say their child has 'grown out of' eczema but now they have asthma, or tummy aches and loose bowels, or catarrh. When we advise stopping the dairy again, the symptoms disappear again. We have seen this over and over again, from babies to children to adults.

The same tension can be felt in people who are sensitive

to wheat, pollen, nuts, dust, egg and a whole host of other substances. I am not sure whether the feeling we feel could be picked up by a machine, but I suspect not. After all, what we feel is a distortion in the flow of life force.

These tensions tell us what substances a person has difficulties with but they often point us to how they became a problem in the first place and also what has to be done to clear the problem. Food issues are certainly increasing and we think we know a reason why.

How sensitivities may be created

Our working hypothesis goes like this. If you eat a substance after an event that caused you to be upset, your body makes a connection between the substance and the upset. I know the body is capable of doing this - I still smell vomit any time I drink cider, from over-indulging when too young to handle alcohol. If the upset isn't sorted out, whenever you eat that substance your mind brings up that connection and causes you to be tense and have digestive problems, at least. Other people can notice this problem after food poisoning. Sometimes it is very difficult to eat the food that caused the food poisoning.

This body memory of remembering past 'mistakes' with food can be useful to remind you those particular mushrooms should be avoided or shellfish should be eaten fresh. And so you can learn which food is good for you and which isn't. Nowadays, we eat quite mindlessly, even while watching television, for example. And because we eat so mindlessly, how does our mind know that the harrowing scene on television isn't a real-life experience? Television has been known to raise our heart rate, blood pressure, anxiety levels, and a whole host of other physiological responses. I don't think watching television while eating has alone caused the massive increase in food sensitivities but it hasn't helped.

In the past, people used to bless their food. That ritual lost its energetic power when it became a series of words, parroted until virtually meaningless. The idea that you can look at your food and bring your thoughts and feelings to a still point might be the original reason for the blessing. If it was, I could see how it would be useful. And, of course, being truly grateful for something is the magical formula for allowing it to continue.

What we do when presented with a sensitivity

As I have said, when a patient presents with an emotional problem or trauma we use a trauma-ticket. This is a piece of paper that in some way represents the patient's problem and we use that to stimulate a response in order to undo the problem, as explained in Chapter 7: Processing an event or trauma.

When a patient comes to me with a substance sensitivity I use the substance as the trauma ticket. The problem substance is placed on the person and before it stays there for too long and cause overwhelm, I get hold of some of the tension created and take it to a still point. The substance is usually contained in a small glass bottle but the body is sensitive enough to create a reaction I can feel and work with. I proceed in this way until the substance no longer causes a reaction. With most food sensitivities this means the person can now eat the food freely with no more physical reactions. Extra caution is taken with life-threatening allergies such as nuts - see below.

As you can see, the method of removing a sensitivity to a physical substance is virtually the same as removing an emotional or mental one. We use a representation of the problem to stimulate a controllable reaction in the person, undo that small reaction and repeat until the whole problem is resolved. Actually, the same is true for physical problems such as strains, sprains, osteoarthritis and all kinds of injuries.

Ingesting inappropriate substances

Ingesting inappropriate substances is probably the single worst thing people do for their health, especially since most people have lost the ability to determine what is good for them and what isn't. In the past, people used to bless their food. Blessing the food also gives you a bit more time for your mind to consider what you are eating. Using your life force to determine which foods create a dance and which a still point would quickly determine which foods are good for you and which aren't. The blanket 'broccoli is good for you', or whatever the in vogue vegetable is, is not true for everyone. Children are often considered fussy eaters but they are probably more in tune with their needs than adults. The exception to this tends to be sugar and fast food where the ego will tell you it is good for you when it might not be.

It is possible to use the life force to help with the task of knowing what you need and what you should avoid. Without the life force you have to go on the word of other people who are working from their own theory rather than feeling what is going on. The point is that, at any given time, every single person has different requirements and while most poisonous mushrooms, for example, will remain poisonous for everyone, some people may need something that others would find detrimental. Being able to feel the life force, and what disturbs it, is the solution to this problem.

Can you stop people being allergic to nuts?

Being allergic to anything can clearly be dangerous. Many people have died from having an allergic reaction. This shows how much power the life force and I-force.hold. What is the solution?

One way of solving allergy problems is to simulate the problem in a small way and teach the patient's body how to deal with that. Western medicine tries to do this with desensitisation therapy. Without the life force, though, the mechanism behind the body's reaction won't be understood and it will be a hit and miss affair, if not actually dangerous.

All allergic reactions are the life force/I-force playing out their battle and we have a certain amount of control over these forces but not an unlimited amount. What we can do is expose the patient to an amount of the allergen that we can comfortably deal with and show the patient's life force and I-force how to deal with that amount. Each time we make sure the patient can deal with that amount of exposure before we move on to a greater exposure. Initially, we keep the substance in a stoppered glass bottle and put it on their clothed stomach. There is a felt reaction and when that is completely resolved, and this can take a few sessions, no further reaction can be felt. At this point, with most food sensitivities, the person can now eat that food with no more problems. With severe nut allergies (where someone carries an epipen) we may continue the treatment more cautiously. We might take the nut out of the bottle but still keep it on the clothed stomach. We keep the clearing of the problem going by moving from the clothed stomached to the unclothed hand then, arm, upper arm, cheek, chin and eventually lips. Each time we feel the effects of the nuts, or other substance, and each time teach the person how to deal with the reaction.

Eventually, we get to the lips and tongue, this can take a few sessions but is always checked on the next appointment before advancing the substance closer to the mouth. The patient by this time has understood what we are doing and invariably wants to get on with procedure as fast as possible. Our job is to make sure every stage is sorted out and we go back over various areas with different nuts, just to be clear. Actually, I have never claimed the patient has stopped being allergic but they can feel what we do and they understand how they can deal with exposure to problem substances. This is how we may deal with an extreme allergy, but the vast majority of people who come to us only need four or five sessions to clear all their sensitivities.

Cow's milk & dairy products

All mammals feed their babies a milk that provides every nutrient their offspring needs. It is a dynamic fluid given from one living creature to another, still warm and full of useful bioactive molecules that promote a healthy microbiome and protect against infection and disease. Human milk production responds to the baby's needs as it grows, changing from the initial colostrum to baby milk to milk suitable for a toddler.

Cow's milk is perfectly formulated to help a baby calf grow into a large bovine. How has the confusion between cow and human happened? My experience tells me that cow's milk is most unsuitable for humans at any stage of life. The proteins in cow's milk are not easy for a human to digest and cause all manner of health problems. Lactose is also a problem for people in many parts of the world who lack the lactase enzyme needed to digest it. But the most common problem comes from the protein, which is found in all cow's milk and dairy products and is often added to foods in the form of (skimmed) milk protein or casein. Most ready meals, sauces, processed foods and even biscuits have milk protein in them.

What harm can dairy products do?

Dairy products are generally considered a vital part of our diet and people think they must be good for us, but they cause all kinds of symptoms, including eczema, acne, headaches, migraines, baby colic, IBS (bloating, wind, loose stools, 'abdominal migraines'/ tummy aches nausea and vomiting), asthma, ENT (ears, nose and throat conditions, including glue ear, inflamed tonsils and adenoids), catarrh, rhinitis, sinusitis, post-nasal drip, chronic cough, brain fog, irritability, tiredness and low mood.

It is estimated that 1 in 5 children and 1 in 12 adults have eczema, which is almost exclusively caused by milk protein. Every year 5 million people in the UK visit their GP with 'nasal blockage', most often caused by milk products.

Most of us are born unable to deal well with cow's milk and this sensitivity continues until we die. If one or both parents have the sensitivity then it is most likely that all their children will inherit it. Not all their children may suffer equally but it is usually a mistake to assume it is only one of the children who has to be singled out for special treatment and put on a dairy-free diet. They are labelled as the sickly child, or the one with a problem, which is unfair on the child and the wrong way to look at milk sensitivity. It is not the child who is unhealthy - they are usually perfectly healthy so long as they avoid dairy - but it is their diet that is wrong. It is nearly always the wrong diet for the rest of the family too, and they will benefit from all of them avoiding milk and dairy products together. When they do, the parents often find that symptoms they or the other children had before disappear and they all feel better for it.

Different members of the same family can have a whole range of symptoms that all come from milk protein sensitivity.

Do not assume that when a child appears to grow out of eczema that they can now cope well with milk. They will almost certainly develop other symptoms sooner or later.

Symptoms can come and go throughout life, with some people getting acne in their twenties instead of their teens and other people getting eczema or post-nasal drip (often leading to a chronic cough) for the first time when they are older. These symptoms are created by the body as it tries to clear the milk proteins from the system, and will stop when dairy is eliminated from the diet. How do I know? Because I can feel dairy products distorting the flow of life force in another person.

Migraines are interesting because in women they often start at puberty and end with menopause, leading people to conclude they are hormonal. The hormonal cycle clearly creates an additional stress on the body, but in most cases when the offending food or drink item is eliminated, the migraines stop, even when the hormonal cycle continues. From our testing, milk and dairy products are the most common cause of migraine, but others are tea, wheat and over-cooked oils, depending on the person's sensitivity.

Isn't milk good for me?

The Milk Marketing Board, established in 1933 and dissolved in 2002, did a fantastic job over nearly 70 years in persuading us that cow's milk is some kind of superfood. It is, for calves. A calf needs to grow 1,000 lbs in its first year. Cow's milk is perfect for turning baby cows into big, protein-packed lumbering cattle who chew the cud while staring vacantly into space. This doesn't mean people need to 'drinka pinta milka day' as the Board successfully persuaded us to do for many years.

We have our own human milk for our babies, which is perfectly designed to nourish a human baby until it can eat the full range of solids to get its nutrients. At no point is cow's milk 'needed' or beneficial to a baby or young child, unless they are deprived of human milk as a young baby, or have insufficient nutrition from solids when weaned.

This may sound brutal to mothers who are unable to feed their babies with their own milk, but it doesn't help us to fudge the basic facts. We cannot pretend that cow's milk formula is just as good as breast milk, because that would be a lie.

Cow's milk and dairy products are so often treated as an essential and healthy part of our diet when in reality they are unnecessary and cause many problems for our bodies.

It doesn't matter how many 'essential nutrients' cow's milk may or may not contain; if it is bad for you then you don't want to be consuming it. Also, just because these nutrients exist in the milk doesn't mean that we can get at them since we have a very different digestive system from cows.

Calcium is a good example of this. There is calcium in milk but we can't benefit from it much as it comes without the necessary magnesium to metabolise it.

Osteoporosis & Calcium

I have treated many women (and the occasional man) who have osteoporosis (bone thinning) despite every single one of them eating milk and dairy products on a daily basis all their lives. They usually have a problem absorbing calcium rather than a lack of it in their diet. (This absorption problem can nearly always be corrected using the Boulderstone Technique.)

A much better source of calcium is green vegetables, which come complete with the required magnesium. Cows mainly eat grasses (containing calcium) to make milk for their babies but also to sustain themselves. Nuts, seeds, fish and seafood are also good sources of calcium. I have to say, though, that I rarely find people are short of calcium (including people who never eat dairy) unless there is an absorbency problem.

The RDA (Recommended Daily Allowance) for calcium in the USA is twice as much as in Japan. How much is this influenced by lobbying by the dairy industry?

There is a prevalent myth that menopausal women need to consume cow's milk for the calcium to prevent osteoporosis. However, we put most of the calcium on to our bones before the age of 35. After that the main issue is with keeping calcium in our bones and stopping it leaching out. It tends to leach out when we eat too many acidic foods, such as dairy (!) or too much animal protein (dairy again). Tea and coffee are also highly acidic. As calcium is alkali, the body will release it from our bones in order to neutralise the acidity levels in the blood. The answer (as usual) lies with plenty of green vegetables to keep the body as alkaline as possible

Some people with osteoporosis are prescribed calcium tablets together with alendronic acid which forces calcium on to the bones, making them somewhat denser, but also risks making them more brittle and therefore more likely to break.

The countries with the highest number of hip fracture (a measure of osteoporosis) are the same countries with high milk consumption: Scandinavia, Northern Europe, USA. Much lower levels of both osteoporosis and milk consumption are found in Asia and even lower in Africa.

The Boulderstone Technique can help if the body is not absorbing calcium properly, and also if there are issues with manufacturing vitamin D, and issues with oestrogen. These issues are often present in people diagnosed with osteoporosis, or heading in that direction.

Further studies

The symptoms of dairy sensitivity listed above are well known and are clearly the result of the body trying to clear out the protein molecules. This is similar to the sneezing and mucous the body produces to try and clear from the body problematic particles of dust, pollens or an unwanted virus. More serious effects that consumption of dairy may have on the body are not studied as much as they should be, probably because it would be directly opposed to the interests of the pharmaceutical industries and they would never fund it.

However, there are several studies that link milk consumption with cancer e.g. The China Study by Campbell & Campbell. A glass of milk a day increases your chances of developing prostatic or ovarian cancer by 300%, according to a study done by nurses in Maryland. A recent study in Norway showed an increase in the incidence of breast cancer in women who drank more milk than the control group.

Psychological attachment to milk

Every February a bovine beauty contest takes place in Verden an der Aller, North-West Germany. The winner last year was 'Madame the milk cow', judged to be the prettiest cow in the country, praised for her winning attributes of a beautiful udder, good teat placement, solid footing and broad pelvis.

This fetishisation of dairy cows is not confined to

Germany, although it may be particularly strong in Northern Europe where we have good pasture for grazing and depend greatly on milk and cheese in our diets.

Our psychological attachment to milk starts with our physical attachment to our mothers during conception and pregnancy. When we are born we continue to attach ourselves to our mother's body through breast-feeding. This is a bonding process which also gives us all the nourishment we need. When a plastic bottle of cow's milk formula is given in place of breast-feeding we naturally get attached to this. This can happen from birth or at any point when breast milk is replaced by cow's milk in some form. Young children become very attached to their bottles and often insist on having their milk. It is no surprise that from a young age we see cow's milk as essential when it may have been the only substance given us to keep us alive as babies, and is associated with Mother. In a sense we confuse it with mother's milk and this confusion causes problems throughout the body and throughout our lives.

So often when I tell a patient that they have a problem with cow's milk, they will say 'but I must have **my** milk; I can't live without it; I love dairy products' etc.

Parents often describe their children as being 'addicted to milk'. They crave it and demand it. On closer questioning we often discover that they started off refusing milk and had an aversion to it - because it caused them problems. The well-meaning parents forced them to drink it, often by disguising it with sugar, chocolate and other flavours. The natural aversion then becomes a craving. Sometimes children crave foods that give them a bit of a buzz, a mild drug-like effect, as their body reacts to it. This is in addition to the association with being nurtured by the primary care-giver.

We are indoctrinated to believe that milk is not only good for us but an essential food for our survival. The cow becomes our substitute mother or wet nurse.

There is even a pervasive idea that babies should be weaned off the breast by 6 months (or 10 months in anthroposophical circles) in order to be put on to Mother Cow. This seems to be the dominant ideology amongst new mothers, their health visitors and doctors currently. It goes completely against the World Health Organisation's recommendation that babies should be breast-fed for at least two years. They also note that the world average to stop breast feeding is at the age of four.

People are disgusted by the idea of dairy products made from human breast milk, although ice cream made from human milk does exist now. What I find even more surprising is how people react when I tell them they may be able to tolerate sheep's milk cheese or yoghurt. Some practically gag at the idea. Yet somehow drinking milk from a cow is not seen as distasteful in the least, as that is thought of as just normal milk, almost as if it comes from a factory, not an animal.

The Boulderstone Technique can undo many food sensitivities but we have found it impossible to remove a dairy problem. We see this as proof that dairy should not be consumed.

Coffee, tea and migraines

Even being a reasonably sensitive person it took me over 20 years to discover that coffee was not good for me. It was one of the things that sent my mind out of control making it difficult to think. I gave up coffee but like a boomerang it kept coming back into my life and continued to cause more havoc. One of the problems is that the havoc it causes isn't permanent and doesn't affect too many other people. That doesn't stop coffee causing many people problems and I would say that *everyone* that drinks coffee daily is sleep deprived. Many people report that when they stop coffee they get a headache or migraine that can last a few days. By drinking coffee people put off that headache and for at least this reason it is addictive.

One of the things coffee does is make you more mentally sharp than you would be if you hadn't had it. This conceals a hidden problem, especially if you get used to and familiar with this feeling. Through meditation and my work I have noticed what I would call the 'established behaviour pattern'. In this pattern people grow towards the way they are. Happy people tend to stay happy, miserable people tend to stay miserable. Coffee-hyped people are mentally sharp and stay mentally sharp, while they have coffee. When their coffee consumption slows down so do they. Fifty years of coffee consumption is not a small amount and could be in excess of 100,000 cups. It will leave the consumer needing coffee to stay functioning normally. If they do not get their 'fix' they will experience the opposite of the mental sharpness they used to experience when first starting out. Sometimes the opposite is true and you can see a reformed alcoholic, who hasn't drunk anything, slurring words, lacking co-ordination and confused. This is damage that may be treatable.

Tea is another drug that appears to give people headaches when they stop drinking it. I discovered that people that drink six or more mugs a day generally get headaches, sometimes migraines, that go away a week or so after stopping the tea. I would say that there have been hundreds of patients who I have seen who have had migraines that disappeared after they stopped tea. Those same people were prescribed some crazy drug by a doctor to take when they had a migraine which rarely worked. There is something wrong with tea.

Asthma, eczema and acne

Asthma and eczema are connected and often seen together. The skin is an organ of elimination, removing waste liquids as well as gasses. The skin is also a barrier to the environment. The lungs also form a barrier to the environment and is the major organ dealing with gas exchange.

Eczema can come about because the skin is trying to eliminate something through the pores that somehow gets stuck or hung up. In this case the skin first of all gets inflamed. You can see this in people when the skin first gets dry and has slightly raised bumps. As conditions get worse the bumps join together and become red sore patches, very often in places that sweat more easily, where skin folds over itself, such as inside the elbows and wrists. This is when the skin needs to break down to eliminate the difficult substance. It is also itchy at this point wanting to be scratched to allow the particles to be removed. The Western Medical solution is to use a steroid cream. This doesn't cure the problem even if it gets the skin temporarily clearer. The solution is to stop ingesting the substance that the skin is trying to eliminate. Putting something on the outside is never going to solve the problem but this is pretty much all Western medicine offers.

The most common substance that needs eliminating is dairy and in many cases I have seen improvement within days of dairy being removed from the diet. Of course, dairy products aren't the only substance that gets caught in the skin but whatever the substance is it will cause a distortion in the flow of life force and can be felt by a practitioner. Once the offending substance has been removed from the diet the eczema generally clears up. We have treated literally thousands of cases in this way.

Asthma is a similar story. Remove the dairy from the diet and the asthma often goes away or at least is much reduced. If environmental allergens such as dust, feathers, mould, pollens and animal dander are causing asthma then all of these sensitivities can be removed by the Boulderstone Technique. No need for steroid sprays. I had a childhood friend that died from an asthma attack. Would he have been saved if dairy, or whatever caused his problem, had been eliminated? I don't know but being so arrogant that you don't even bother to check it out, which is the current state of Western medicine, is pretty much unforgivable.

Acne is another condition that often yields to discovering the offending food stuff and eliminating it or clearing it, dairy being the most common offender. Giving antibiotics that do horrendous damage for years after taking them for acne makes me think less of doctors.

Since the Boulderstone Technique can't remove the bad effects of consuming dairy products we advise eliminating them.

Vitamin and mineral absorption

Most patients we see are getting enough vitamins and minerals in their diet, but sometimes they are not absorbing them easily. Using the Boulderstone Technique we can educate the body to accept the substance or substances that it has been rejecting. People often have a problem absorbing one (and sometimes more than one) of the following: iron, vitamin B12, magnesium, chromium, calcium, vitamin D, iodine, other B vitamins. This absorbency issue can lead to various symptoms like anaemia, exhaustion, nervous system issues, insomnia, blood sugar problems, osteopoenia and osteoporosis, thyroid issues etc. These symptoms disappear when the cause has been addressed and people start absorbing the nutrition they need from their food.

Hormones

What do hormones do? They change your body. They change your growth and development, they speed your body functions, they are actively involved in sexual function, they are actively involved in having a child, they change your mental state, they change your physical and emotional state. And what does the ego want? It wants control and stability. Human egos tend to resist change and so we try to stop the changes or at least change their speed. Is it any wonder we resist the effect of hormones?

It is easy to understand. Why would anyone want to grow old? Generally, they wouldn't, and so they think the way to stay young is to take hormones. You can see world leaders not grow old like other people - hormones. You can see people with phenomenally big muscles - hormones. You can see middle aged women dressed up as if they were still 18 - hormones. Hormones are used to suppress pregnancy and promote it and to allow diabetics to eat sugar. Hormones change your body and give a bit more freedom to your ego, at a price. It's always at a price.

In a similar way to rejecting essential nutrients, the body can seem to set up an opposition to its own hormones. A prime example of this is insulin resistance. We can feel when a person has insulin resistance as they react to insulin in a similar way to a food sensitivity. They are no longer responding to the hormone normally and they are likely to have blood sugar issues such as type 2 diabetes or pre-diabetes. The Boulderstone Technique can restore a person's relationship to their own insulin so that they can respond to it as needed and not have to over-produce it.

Similarly, if someone isn't responding to one or more of their thyroid hormones then they are most likely to develop thyroid problems such as under-active or overactive thyroid. With fertility hormones like oestrogen and progesterone, all kinds of symptoms can be caused by a lack of normal response to the hormone by the body: fertility issues, menstrual cycle disorders, fibroids, cancer, polycystic ovaries, endometriosis etc.

When people overeat there are often emotional issues to address, but physically they are often not responding properly to their leptin and/or ghrelin appetite-regulating hormones. Educating the body on these can really change a person's relationship to food.

The problematic reacting to your own hormones has to be undone by working with the life force and I-force, not by prescribing more hormones. Blaming the hormones will not get you anywhere: the problem is how you react to them. This can be resolved using the Boulderstone Technique.

Chapter 9: The still point

The still point won't happen because you tell it to; it is not a construction of the ego. It only exists when the ego goes quiet and has nothing to say. So every prejudice has been dropped and every reason to be something other than you are has evaporated. In my opinion, the fastest way to a still point is with the help of another person using the Boulderstone Technique. Alternatively, if you are on your own, a good way is through meditation. There are many ways to a still point. The still point, as a concept, is talked about in other cultures and is called mushin in Japanese, samadhi in Hindi, fana in Sufism and flow state in Western philosophy

As a result of trauma, lack of role models or pain, many people find getting to a still point challenging and they are forced to live in the world of the ego. Living exclusively in the world of the ego is a wholly unsatisfactory experience because you never deal with the reality of things and can never totally let go. Instead you are dealing with the superficial, the gloss, the man made, and the facade of things. As far as health is concerned that means you look at the symptoms of diseases and not their causes.

There are consequences to dealing with symptoms instead of causes

When Western medicine chose to deal with the symptoms of an illness rather than the cause it slowly brought to the fore a whole train of unfortunate problems. The first of these is that every illness treated for its symptoms will never be cured even if the symptoms are ameliorated. Any illness that can't produce the symptoms it wants to will produce symptoms that are worse for the patient.

Example 1: Taking a painkiller for a headache.

How does taking a painkiller for a headache make the headache worse? The headache is a symptom not a cause and taking a painkiller for the headache (actually, they rarely work anyway) does nothing for the reason you got the headache in the first place. The reason could be any number of problems: lack of water, stress from work, too much chocolate or even a brain tumour. The list goes on but the point is the painkiller does nothing for those problems, only perhaps for the symptom. In fact, the pill stops you having to think about the cause and allows the problem to continue.

Example 2: Putting steroid cream on eczema.

My belief is that eczema, in many cases, is caused by inappropriate food substances the body attempts to excrete through the skin. When that is the case, applying steroid cream does nothing for the problem. The real solution is to find the food causing the problem and probably eliminate it from the diet. If the steroid cream works, and it clears up the skin , it doesn't solve the problem. The patient will eat the substance again, cause a new skin issue and require a repeat prescription of steroids. Unfortunately, the steroid cream also damages the skin! The patient does not do well out of this situation.

Who benefits from treating symptoms instead of causes?

Asking yourself who does this benefit will bring you face to face with an ugly truth. Clearly, if disease is never cured, the people who make the pills will financially benefit. Doctors will benefit by being in almost permanent demand. The hospital will always be under pressure and always need to be expanded. The National Health Service in the UK is already the largest employer in Europe, creating 1.5 million full time jobs but it will always need more people because it never gets to the core of any illness. When you stop natural symptoms from occurring, unnatural ones present themselves.

Treating symptoms and not the causes of the problem is a mistake not confined to healthcare and is pervasive in the Western world. From dentists to car mechanics to teachers and more, looking superficially at a problem and solving that symptom makes more money and keeps people employed for longer.

Governments, also, deal with symptoms rather than causes, looking at short term gains and political expediency to secure election victories rather than unpopular but more efficient solutions. This is one consequence of having elections every few years. Having governments in power for even longer, though, is another example of dealing with symptoms rather than causes. The only real solution is always a still point but, for me at least, I don't yet know how to implement a still point at governmental level.

Doctors get between you and your health. Doctors could be advisors and that is how they started out but it all went pear-shaped for patients when doctors took over control. Doctors still claim to be advisors but that has actually changed now. Instead they are much more dictatorial, assuming you are not clever enough to work out your own solutions. They have made the disease process much more complicated by employing laboratories, scientists, elaborate machinery and electronics, not to cure but to diagnose. And the diagnosis they come up with might be accurate as far as it goes but it is never the whole story. After all, they don't measure health. What they do with their diagnosis is medicate, to remove a symptom, leaving you to deal with the real illness. No medication has ever cured, even if it removes the symptom.

The solution

There is a solution to any human problem, health or otherwise, and it is in your hands. To solve any problem you have to get in contact with the still point. Your life force has been with you every step you have taken and gone down every path you have gone down, without your ego confusing it. It knows you. Any symptoms you experience are as a result of the life force and I-force conflicting. And by getting your ego and I-force out of the way, you will find the real cause of those symptoms. Don't call the life force God, call it life force. Keep your beliefs about God to yourself as it does not help anybody to impose them on someone else.

If you think you can't yet feel your life force, get someone to help you. Remember to trust your body. Your body speaks to you with symptoms. Listen to what they are trying to say rather than cover them up with painkillers and other drugs. Sometimes you may misinterpret them and this will be because your ego gets in the way. However, if you have to take a painkiller to stop being overwhelmed, do so. If you don't understand what a symptom is telling you, work a little harder. Your body gave you those symptoms because it knows you can work it out. You might not like the answer but your body doesn't lie. Also remember that a solution lies in your hands. You do not have to go elsewhere or speak to or confront anyone else to sort out any problem. You have in your possession one of the most precious instruments in the world that you can't buy, regardless of how much money you have. You are your own best doctor, but only when you listen.

If you feel rough after a night of drinking then your body is just responding to what you have done. The symptoms are there to inform you that drinking in this way is not good for you. You are not being punished by your body, you are being informed. The thought that you are being punished is a childish thought and separates you from your body. This is what the ego does, it separates you from your self. Not responding to what your body tells you, tells your body it is not talking loud enough and it will turn up the volume. That is why it is so important to listen. If you can't understand what it is saying then tell it and listen in the quiet moments, in dreams and while in nature.

When you bring any symptom into contact with a still point the symptom will wriggle and contort but if you keep hold of the still point you will become aware of the cause of the symptom. By holding on to the still point the ego goes quiet. The awareness of the cause of the symptom might not come in words for it will be in the language of 'knowing' (See Appendix: The language of 'knowing'). As you hold on to the still point, pain will become sensation and fears and worries evaporate. While you stay in a still point healing takes place, for the ego can no longer get in the way.

Finding the cause

Finding the cause of illness is essential and no one can do that for you because the cause is always unique to the individual. For example, it is a choice to believe that nothing happens after somebody dies; that there is no after-life. A consequence of that belief can be that when someone close to you dies, their death, and also their life, can appear meaningless. Depression can result. The cause of the depression, is the belief that nothing happens after death coupled with the question 'What is the point of life?' Those thoughts create an inner battle. It must be obvious that the inner battle is never going to be changed with antidepressants but, of course, that is what most often gets prescribed. Finding the real cause of the depression can be a difficult task because you are in the middle of the symptom: depression. The only way to finding the cause is through a still point. It is only when you are fully at peace that you will realise what is going on, that the problematic belief is a choice. It doesn't matter what anybody says, that choice won't be changed by anyone but you. The solution is unique to you.

Whether someone has an after-life or not is actually irrelevant. The problem is the rigid belief that everyone doesn't have an after-life coupled with other personal beliefs that then create a conflict.

Being diagnosed with a disease, like depression, doesn't change the cause of the illness. In order to cure, the cause needs to be found and that cause won't always exist in words. The cause will only be found when the ego goes quiet, in a still point.

If you have an accident in your car and you can't get it out of your mind, when it is time to travel in your car again you may well be conflicted. Your anxiety is the playing out of your inner battle. Taking anti-anxiety medication doesn't get to the cause but getting to a still point will force you to confront the real issue. Your ego might not want you to do that and if you don't, then you will keep your anxiety.

It doesn't matter what anyone says, their words don't change the truth. The thought that someone saying something to you can upset you and distort your flow of life force, without your collusion, is preposterous. You can take offence at what someone says but that is a choice. The idea that getting upset is solely your responsibility isn't a fashionable view.

Inner contradiction, and inner battles, are the basis of all acquired mental and emotional issues (as explained in

Chapter 5) but are always cleared with a still point, which happens without words or talking.

This still point is the only complete solution. Blocking thoughts, taking medication, counselling, avoidance techniques, violence or other mind games will not cure. Actually, they keep the problem in place.

The solution to every problem is the still point. Even before you are aware of a problem the solution is the still point.

The best way to a still point is through meditation. However, if you have a broken leg, go to the hospital.

Meditation

Meditation is the single most important thing you can do for your physical, mental and emotional health because it shows you all the distortions in your flow of life force. People might say they can't meditate because their mind gets distracted but those distractions are what meditation is meant to show you. That is the point of meditation. Distractions point directly to the distortions in the flow of life force which are the sources of your illnesses. If you process the distractions you are left with a still point.

Every illness is caused by a distortion in the flow of life force and silent meditation will show you every distortion. Of course bugs and viruses are involved in diseases but bugs and viruses can only get a foothold if there is a distortion in the flow of life force.

Guided meditations, prayer, whale sounds and other aids to meditation can lead to personal discoveries but eventually they become an encumbrance. The idea of all meditation, whether guided or not, is to show you where your distortions are and allow you to work through them. You have less to distract you in silent meditation and so you will discover distortions more easily.

Starting meditation

You can start by sitting and going quiet. Do you get distracted with thoughts very quickly? You have to decide if you need to take a break and sort out those distractions or ignore them. You can stay focussed by doing any number of things from counting your breath to chanting a mantra, either out loud or internally, listening to whale noises or a commercially produced meditation aid, but all these techniques need to be dropped as soon as possible. The best way forward is to use the lightest touch that allows you to stay focussed and mindful. Anything that doesn't need an outside source is best, like counting your breathing, for example. Count your breath from one to ten and then start back at one. When that has been achieved without getting distracted, count to one hundred. When you can do that without effort, drop the counting. Choose the lightest touch that works. Remember distractions come from a distortion in the flow of life force and need to be processed and can't be ignored. If you ignore them they will get stronger.

Sometimes major difficulties arise. Find a way to solve them. It's always possible, for you created your difficulties in the first place. You may see external events as being the cause but if you look more closely you will find it is your reaction to those external events that causes the problem. By all means read about how others solved their problems but their solutions will only partially work for you. Realise all problems are solvable, otherwise they aren't problems.

All illnesses (distortions) succumb to the still point. Given a still point and absolutely any problem and the still point will always see out the distortion. Every problem is sortable.

All meditation instruction that is aimed at only getting

you to a still point will ultimately make meditation more difficult. The still point exists in you and is covered over with ego layers. The still point will appear as a result of meditation but only because you have processed the layers.

This is the only meditation instruction you will ever need (apart from the 21 day meditation course in the Appendix). But you might need help with a particular distortion or difficulty. If you seek out that help, the Boulderstone Technique works well!

Nature: another way to a still point

You don't need to be perfect to get to a still point. You can get there by overwhelming your ego. This is how drugs work, although they are not recommended. One of the best ways of reaching a still point while not being perfect is to be in nature. What is it about nature that makes it so special? Certainly nature has the ability to quieten thoughts through its unfathomability. Driving home today I saw a landscape of fields and trees. There were so many trees it would be impossible for me to count them. The same was true for the number of fields. Perhaps it is because I used to be a mathematics teacher but when I think about the number of leaves on a tree and realise I can't count them and combine that with the uncountable trees, I am left in awe. My thinking stops, it's got nowhere to go. I know it isn't like this for everyone and it isn't always like this for me but it was today. I reached a still point just by being in nature. That is significant because when you reach a still point you can't be unhappy, or sad or depressed or anxious, you are just one with the universe. And when you bring a difficulty together with a still point the difficulty gets resolved.

STILL POINT

Boulderstone Technique

Distortion

Appendix

What's it like to be a Boulderstone Technique therapist

If you could take on another person's illness would you? If you could feel the distortion in the flow of their life force, the cause of their illness, would you? Would you take it on in its entirety, as if it were yours? You might get stuck with it.

When I first started on this path, taking on other people's illnesses is what happened and it still happens today, sometimes. Because of the way we work we have to tune into the life force of another person using our own life force. Their distortion becomes our distortion and sometimes we take it home with us and sometimes it even takes a few days to get completely clear of it. But, so far, we do get rid of it and doing so always makes us stronger. For we then know how to deal with another illness. Four decades later, I must have worked through tens of thousands of illnesses. I still haven't cleared everything but there aren't many things that feel new.

Connection

To understand the Boulderstone Technique you first have to understand the connection we make with another human being. Whenever you really connect with a work of art you see something that lies beyond your five senses. A painting is just a collection of colours arranged in a unique way, a song is just a bunch of notes and words arranged in a unique way. What takes it beyond the five senses is your interpretation aided by whatever the artist was going through when they painted the picture or wrote the song. Somehow the human part gets through. When you see past the colours and words you make a connection with the life force of the artist. This may be haunting, tragic, uplifting, happy, or any other feeling that is unmeasurable and lost to science.

A human being is their own work of art. They have experienced incredible feelings, been stuck inside a womb for forty weeks, been birthed, had frustrating parents that couldn't understand them, been starved, overfed, allowed to lie in their own piss and shit, been assaulted by sounds, smothered by smells, had needles stuck into them and all that before they are a week old!

All experiences have to be assimilated. When they aren't it is because the I-force is resisting and causing a distortion in the flow of life force and, therefore, symptoms.

A human being, of any age, is still their own work of art and as a Boulderstone Technique practitioner you have to see beyond their colours and words. Somehow, the human part of the patient must get through so the practitioner can connect with the illness. But you can only see a patient when you are clear, when your issues and problems aren't making themselves known. But when you do connect you can feel the distortion in the flow of life force and then you can move on to clearing.

Every single symptom a patient has indicates a distortion in the flow of life force and that is what we connect with. So what happens if the patient has cancer or a deep depression? Do we connect with that?

One of the reasons I don't mind taking on another person's distortion in the flow of life force is my belief that I can clear their distortion, whatever it is and wherever it has come from. There are two reasons for this belief.

Firstly, I am usually clear before I start and this means I have little unresolved emotional baggage that will cause their distortion to get stuck in me. Meditation was key here in getting myself as clear as possible.I didn't have a teacher other than being able to know when I was clear and I even got that wrong on a few occasions. I did do various courses: Vipassana 10 day retreats, I spent a month in a dark cave in Thailand, I spoke to a few Buddhist monks in England, I went to see the Dalai Lama in the Albert Hall and learnt how the tarot was a map. I realised that all of that was unnecessary but I had to find that out for myself. It might be different for other people.

Having unresolved baggage is the main reason people pick up illnesses from other people. It is so easy to do so on trains, buses, out in public or if they come into contact with any other human being. You can hide yourself away but it doesn't solve anything and you don't get healthier. You get healthier by overcoming the problems presented by other people, be it their germs or their life difficulties.

Sensitive people are sensitive because they are open and they can get 'infected' from other people, even without physical contact. Most sensitive people know that if they stand next to a person who is upset, for example, they can feel that person's upset. This is how a distortion in the flow of life force is passed on. In most situations the distortion will get cleared fairly quickly, in a matter of seconds, but if the recipient isn't clear within themselves, perhaps they had an argument with their partner, the distortion could stick. Once stuck the body will then need to produce symptoms to get the person to focus on the area that need to be cleared.

The second reason I don't mind taking on another person's distortion is connected to the first. I know that clearing any distortion actually makes me stronger and more able to deal with problems that are similar. When you help other people you are actually helping yourself. In the early days it might have been scary and clearing myself took a huge amount of effort because I was less efficient than I am now. I would go to bed fatigued and wake up fatigued because I was not clear. I used to call it being 'possessed'. Nowadays, clearing is a lot easier and generally happens in seconds. I have cleared so much of my own rubbish. I know there is still more to do but resting in silence has become something more preferable to just about everything else. I wish I had known this when I was growing up.

Medical

Industry

Western

Appendix

The Western medical industry

Every few weeks there is a newspaper article stating that there is a new cure for Multiple Sclerosis or cancer or some other frightening condition. The reason these should be taken with a pinch of salt is because none of them reference the cause of the disease and as such they are only dealing with the symptoms.

The pharmaceutical companies lie when they say vaccinations are 'safe and effective' because they never test them while measuring the health of the person. Therefore it is impossible to say whether they are safe or effective. Vaccinations might well stop the problem they are designed to stop (and even that is questionable) but without measuring the health of the patient before and after taking the vaccine, how is it possible to know they are safe and effective?

Did you know that not one single vaccine has been measured against saline solution? Most vaccines are measured against other vaccines! That is like saying this brand of cigarettes is safe and effective because they are healthier than this other brand. And that passes for science and isn't called out by doctors.

The pharmaceutical companies continue to lie and bribe doctors as proven by the fines that are imposed on them by the courts. In the case of GlaxoSmithKline, in 2012 they were fined $3,000million for, amongst other things, bribing doctors and lying about the effectiveness of their drugs. In 2009 Pfizer were fined $2,300 million for, amongst other misdemeanours, bribing doctors. In 2013 Johnson and Johnson were fined $2,200 million for, amongst other things, lying about the effectiveness of their drugs and bribing doctors. In 2010 AstraZeneca were fined $520 million for, amongst other things, bribing doctors. Now the fines were presumably commensurate with the level of dishonesty and the effects they had on their victims. So for these four pharmaceutical companies to be fined a total of $8 billion is staggering and somehow they are all still in business and making a profit!

A question closer to the cause of the problem is why are doctors taking these bribes? The pharmaceutical companies are handing out these bribes but it only 'works' if the doctors accept them. Why are doctors writing prescriptions that they must know are not in their patients' best interests. I think most patients would be horrified to know they might be getting inferior and/or overpriced medicine from their bribed doctor. Can you tell which doctors are taking bribes? The truth is while any doctor does not dissociate from the doctors that do take bribes surely they are all guilty? How is it possible to trust any doctor that allows his fellow doctors to get away with accepting a bribe?

To put the amounts those four companies were fined into some kind of context, if you could pile $8 billion dollars in $1 dollar bills in one pile it would create a stack 520 miles high, while the edge of space, according to NASA, is only 50 miles above the earth's surface, 520 miles goes well into outer space.

How do these drug companies retain any credibility when they lie about their drugs and bribe doctors? How do doctors retain any credibility when they accept these bribes? Part of the answer to these questions lie in the fact that doctors and pharmaceutical companies have managed to crush any alternative health practices, by claiming they are the only ones using science and, therefore, there is no choice. Bribe taking is often what happens when there is a monopoly. As I have said, one of the reasons alternative therapies are frowned upon by scientists, doctors and most of the press is because of the use of life force and life force can't be measured with instruments and therefore, according to these people, it can't be scientific. Somewhere along the line someone has forgotten that medicine is an art as well as a science.

Another question worth asking is why is there a need to bribe doctors? And why don't the medicines, that are meant to work safely and effectively, sell themselves? Are doctors bribed to keep quiet and in line? Confronted with the choice between a life changing amount of money and lying about whether a vaccine is safe and effective most people would have a difficult decision to make. The trouble is that making the wrong decision just once puts people's health at risk.

When pharmaceutical companies are regularly fined many millions of dollars by the courts, isn't it because this corruption has already taken place? People's lives have been put at risk and, judging by the amount of money these companies have been fined, it must be a substantial risk and involved a lot of people. How is there not a bigger outcry? A significant proportion of the fines goes to the government, so the government profits from pharmaceutical companies bribing doctors. We live in a mad ego-driven world if we want to.

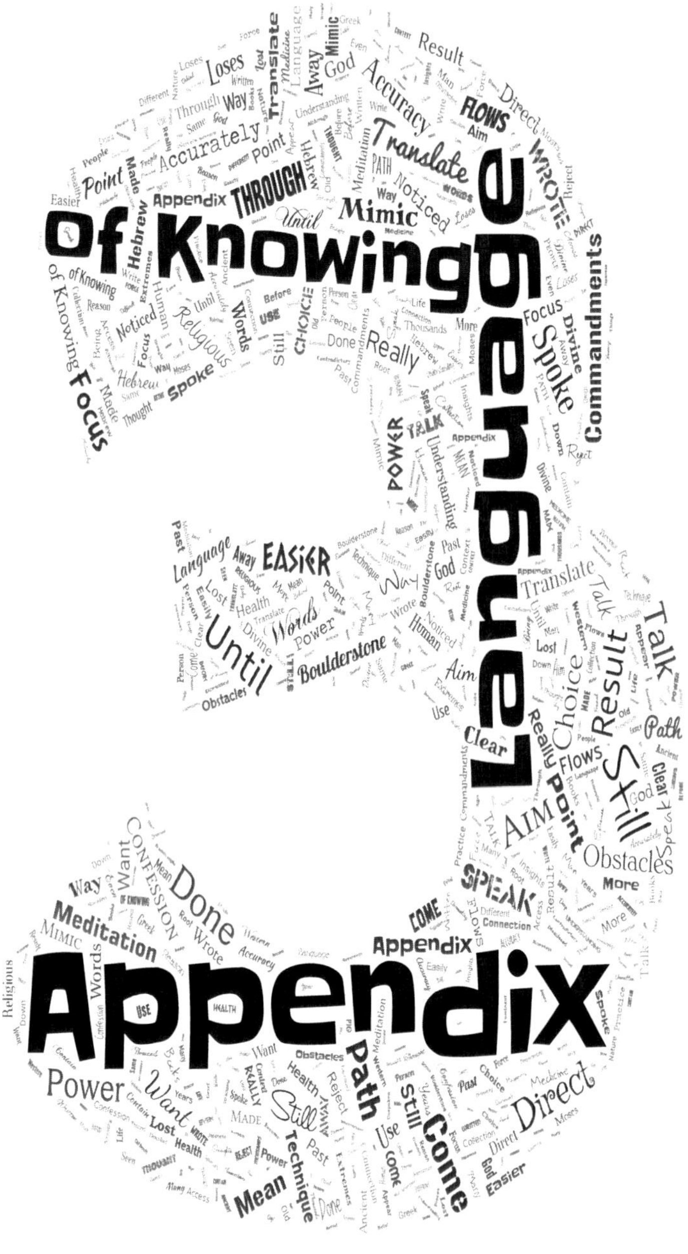
Of Knowing
Language
Appendix

The language of 'knowing'

A lot of what I have written about has been said before, in other languages, in different times and in different ways. They were framed in a poetic or spiritual way and are now rejected as science has become the dominant philosophy. There is, however, little that is new when talking about the health of human beings, even accounting for the 'breakthroughs' of Western Medicine. Understanding what has been written in the past is sometimes difficult when not seen in context and then it is easy to reject. Those writings often go to the very essence of what it is to be a human being but is expressed in an old fashioned way. Our belief that we know more than anyone from the past may be true in some areas but, since our body hasn't changed for thousands of years, old insights often contain extremely useful pieces of knowledge.

The Greeks described the duality of human nature, to find the middle way and avoid extremes. They talked about the power of reason, the nature of grief and loss and to 'know thyself'. Understanding what they were talking about thousands of years ago would help many a person, nowadays.

The Bible is a collection of books from the ancient world that has many deep insights. Some of which might appear to be contradictory but, strangely, that doesn't necessarily make them incorrect because they have to be seen in context. This ancient collection of books was brought together because they were thought to be important but they get dismissed so easily by people who reject religion as non-scientific.

Even our language is useful in understanding how people thought in the past. There is a reason why heal, hale and holy have the same root, and that there is a connection

176

between them. I would throw in a few more words that although they don't have the same root they have a connection. These words are love, happiness, still point, peace, reverence and beauty. They have been lost from Western medicine but not from genuine health. Words can be powerful things but they aren't as powerful as the language of knowing.

If you are not divine you can talk to the divine. When talking to the divine, using a man made language, ie English, Spanish, Latin, Greek, Hebrew, Arabic, Japanese, etc. you may get the answers you seek, but when you use the 'language of knowing', you always get a response. The language of knowing is an unwritten, unspoken language that you already know. It is the thought behind prayer. It often appears to the person that they are talking in their native language but they aren't, for when you come to write it down it can't be done accurately.

When 'translated' into a man made language, the language of knowing loses power. Have you ever noticed that you can more easily get what you want until you speak about it? That is the power of the 'language of knowing', a path direct to God and health. The language flows in the life force. To access it you must be in a still point. When God spoke to Moses he didn't do it in Hebrew, He did it in the 'language of knowing'. When Moses wrote down the commandments from God in Hebrew he had to translate them from the 'language of knowing' to Hebrew and in that translation it lost some of its accuracy. Before words get translated by you into your language of choice they contain life force. After they get translated they can only mimic what you really mean. The language of knowing and the still point is made easier to access through meditation. Confession, and the Boulderstone Technique, can clear away the obstacles to the still point. All religious practices aim for this still point but get lost and focus on the practice rather than the result.

The language of knowing is the language of God.

Appendix 4

Trauma ticket

Trauma

Clean

Steps in trauma clearing

The ideal way to remove PTSD is with a Boulderstone Technique practitioner but not everyone has access to one. The next best way is to attempt it yourself and possibly have a friend to guide and help you. However, there are many things to say before you start and the first is to know that it is possible to make things worse, which is why it is helpful to have an experienced person to help you. However you only make things worse by forcing through a thought or feeling without listening to your own life force.

You must read chapters 1 to 7 of *The Still Point and the Dance* beforehand and understand the principles. You are responsible for your own thoughts and feelings and no one else. If you think otherwise, DO NOT attempt this.

This is a relatively easy process to go through unless it isn't. If it is hard work and you are not seeing progress you are not doing it correctly. Some people understand the technique quickly and some people don't. If you are someone who doesn't get it please do not beat yourself up. You are just looking in the wrong area, you need an experienced person to show you where to look.

Step 1

Find a time when you are not triggered and you feel relatively well in yourself. Trying to sort out trauma in the middle of a panic attack is much more difficult. You need to be able to see yourself objectively at the start of the technique. If that is not possible you need to pick a time when you can.

Step 2

Realise that you can switch on thoughts and feelings about an incident AND switch them off. You are going to do this with a very simple technique. I am going to assume that there is a particular incident that caused your trauma. This is not everyone's experience but it is possible to break down all trauma into a series of separate smaller incidents. It is best to do this and pick only one of those smaller incidents and work with that until it is 100% cleared and then move on to the next. An exception is complex PTSD. If you have cPSTD you need to see a practitioner as this exercise is not for you.

Find a single word (at most two) to represent the traumatising incident and write that word on a piece of paper. Usually, that word is a name but it could be a place or, if the incident is difficult to find, it could be a particular tension in your body. You might need to take some time over this. If there are several names then start with the least problematic.

In my clinic, I always start with the most problematic. The reason for this is that when the patient sees how to deal with the most difficult problem then it gives them the confidence to know that all the other problems are solvable.

You are going to use this 'trauma ticket' to switch your awareness of the trauma on and off.

Step 3

Lie on the floor. The floor is best because you can't accidentally fall off the floor. A bed is not so good because it is associated with sleep and some people use sleep as a way of escaping their problems. What you are going to do is drip-feed your mind with a small bit of your overwhelming trauma and clear that. You do this by placing the trauma ticket on your stomach/chest area. When the trauma ticket is on you, you connect with the trauma. You gather a sufficient amount (I'll talk about what is sufficient in a moment) of the tension and take the trauma ticket off yourself and place it by your side.

Having gathered a small amount of tension, you need to clear it before you move on to the next bit. Every trauma is made up of a number of smaller bits of trauma.

A sufficient amount of trauma to work on is an amount you can clear and an amount that is not overwhelming. Too little and you are wasting your time, too much becomes overwhelming and unworkable. Of course, quantifying a qualitative substance is an art but erring on the side of caution is the way to go. Usually, it takes between five and twenty cycles each lasting about a minute to clear an incident. Of course, this varies and is why seeing a Boulderstone Technique therapist at least once is a good idea.

Step 4

Clearing tension is the heart of the technique. Your body wants you to clear it and your ego doesn't want to be hurt or die. You need to side with your body and trust that it will take you through the problem, a bit at a time. We are not attempting to clear the whole trauma in one go (even if we may clear it in one session). Instead, we are clearing the small piece of it gathered in step 3. Small pieces of trauma are relatively easy to deal with, we do this daily. Examples of small traumas are: stubbing your toe, breaking a plate and coping with bad news. I am sure you are familiar with small traumas. And how do you deal with them? You take them to a still point by embracing them totally and letting their energy dissipate. The bit of trauma you gathered is held and allowed to move around and become boring. One patient I had said 'You bore it to death', and that is what happens. Everything returns to a still point if looked at without getting attached to it. As a large trauma you react to it, you don't have a choice, and by reacting to it you keep it in place. But by splitting it up into small pieces you do have a choice and you can let it dissipate its energy.

Every trauma can be broken down into smaller elements just by gathering smaller pieces. No talking is necessary, you go at your own speed, a coherent timeline is not needed and even a complete narrative is not required. You work with what you feel.

Step 5

Repeat until you reach a still point.

Sometimes people squirrel away a small piece of the trauma and so I ask the question, 'Is the trauma 100% cleared? I am not interested in it being 99% cleared.' If the answer is 'It is 99% sorted' I say, 'That is not good enough. Focus on whatever is remaining and clear that.'

That last bit is often the most difficult to clear but it is important to eradicate all of it otherwise it will still affect your life.

Step 6

Reach a still point.

Appendix 5

A 21 day meditation course

DON'T SKIP AHEAD BECAUSE IT IS GOING TOO SLOWLY. It is meant to be slow, at times, to give you space to think and work things out. Also one day in this course could, in reality, be one hour, one week or one month. Or it could be one day!

Take notes. If you get stuck and have a 21 day log of your efforts you can have a free session with John Boulderstone to get unstuck.

There will be a time when you want to give up or, even worse, forget to do it. If that is the case your ego thinks it knows better. At some point it will realise its error and you will be back where you started. Commit to completing and push through.

There is no one method that will always work, your ego will get to understand it and undermine the method. You have to keep moving on.

Practical issues in meditation

Sitting: You don't have to sit on the floor. It is probably best to sit on the floor but that isn't possible for many people who are not used to it. It is probably best to take the weight of your own spine because distortions held in the spine will show up more easily.

Distractions: If you need to scratch an itch then do so. If you keep having to scratch an itch your body/mind might be trying to distract you. Your body/mind will find many tricks to stop you getting to the cause of your problem and when you finally make that breakthrough there will be no triumphant cry of 'Yes, I've done it.' That is because you will see everything from a whole new perspective where your ego has gone quiet and has accepted the situation. You won't say anything for there is nothing to say.

When applying the Boulderstone Technique I have found the patients's head moves around, sometimes a lot and sometimes very strongly. This is where the patient is processing a difficulty. I see no reason this shouldn't happen while meditating. It doesn't need to move but then again it doesn't need to stay absolutely still. It is possible, once the big issues are out of the way, to meditate in stillness.

Everyone who has a developed ego can meditate. The ego will not like to meditate until you inform it that its rebirth will be better in some way but even then it might not believe you. The only reason people stop meditating is because their ego thinks it knows better. Anyone who has not developed an ego is already meditating.

Day 1:

Read chapter 1 of *The Still Point and the Dance*. If you want more, read it again.

Day 2:

1 x 3 minute meditation. Make this a minimum for every day of the course, you can do more but don't do less. You have to balance the ego desire for control and the life force movement towards peace. That balance goes wrong many times and each time it does your ego dies and is reborn in a more favourable existence. A form of re-incarnation.

Read chapter 9 on meditation. Don't use music, whale sounds or other tricks or other devices. They are not necessary and are only designed to make money. If you keep drifting off, try to analyse why. Try using your breath as a focussing device, if you need to. Count your breath to ten and when you reach ten start back at one. Have low expectations and high motivation. If you keep trying you will always push things on. Sit on the ground, if you are able to without pain or, if you can't, use a chair

Tell your ego what you are doing. If you get your ego on your side it will help you even if it and you believe you are going to die. Listen carefully to its response and resolve its fears, knowing that even if it has to let go and die it will always be reborn. But it will only help you if it thinks by doing so there will be an advantage. Your ego is a wily character.

Day 3:

Read chapter 2. Minimum 3 minute meditation. Make a note of what gets in your way. At some point you will manage to focus for the whole of the three minutes, perhaps by counting your breath up to ten. If you can't, keep going, don't move onto day 4 until you can stay focussed for three minutes.

The next step is to maintain focus while counting your breath up to one hundred. It usually takes about seven minutes. Do not attempt it unless you can easily manage up to ten. Every single attempt at meditation is another step forward. If you move on to the next stage before you are ready it will make everything harder than it needs to be.

Day 4:

Few people manage to count to one hundred in under a week. You can do it with effort but the idea is to make minimum effort. Always meditate with a view to getting to a still point but achieving a hundred focussed breaths is an achievement. Counting at the end of an in-breath is not the same as counting at the beginning of an out-breath. Find out the differences for you. What are the differences? Thoughts tend to start with a new breath but that may or may not be the same for you. One way of counting was certainly easier for me but you have to work with both.

Master the easier way first and then move on to the harder way.

Do not go too fast. When you are at peace you have forever. Speed can lead to your ego winning out and saying something like: 'I can do this easily, I'll have a rest from it.' I noticed that the more effort I put in, the bigger the crash and the longer I stopped for.

Day 5:

Meditate every day, minimum of three minutes. It can be more but not too much. You do not get to put meditation minutes in the bank. Day 5, 6 and 7 consolidate. Go over what you have found difficult.

Write a complete list of all your unresolved emotional problems, and put them in order of severity. Work with number five or, if you haven't got five, the one at the bottom of your list.

Day 6:

Do not look forward in the course. You can't look forward in life, even if you think you can.

Day 7:

Counting to one hundred usually takes about 7 minutes. You can prepare or practise by counting to ten for seven minutes.

Day 8:

This week, check out the 10 Japanese ox-herding pictures which are meant to describe the process you are going through. The ox is meant to represent your mind with the herder the seeker of enlightenment. These pictures are relevant to you if you are meditating for three minutes or you dedicate your whole life to finding a still point. See if you can understand what the artist was trying to depict without reading a commentary. I am sure your explanation will be more relevant to you. Notice that in number 8 the ego has disappeared but you are not at the end of the journey.

Day 9:

Continue to meditate for a minimum of 3 minutes a day. Notice that when you do longer there is less of a desire to meditate the following day. However, you may wish to start meditating morning and evening. You will find that if you meditate in the evening, and manage to clear stuff, your sleep might be better. If you meditate in the morning your day may go better. But your ego gets used to whatever routine you end up with so most of the benefits happen during the change. When you stop meditating you will find your ego will get stronger. Initially, you will like this but inevitably it causes symptoms of some sort. When you resume meditation you can feel righteous. It's best to acknowledge both these feelings and not get attached to either of them.

Day 10:

Keep meditating for a minimum of three minutes. Sometimes push it to twenty minutes. Don't enjoy it or hate it. All you are really doing is clearing out the rubbish that you put in there during the day. When you do a longer meditation you will be clearing out some older stuff. Older stuff is harder but you can take your time. Recognise repeating patterns of distraction and, if you find them difficult to get past, break them down into smaller chunks - whatever that means for you. Every difficult block can be broken down into smaller blocks. When you get past them, notice that they weren't as difficult as you thought. They never are.

Day. 11:

Continue to study the ox-herding pictures. There is a lot in them and they are trying to tell you something. There are other pictorial lessons from other cultures which are more complex but these are kept nice and simple. Meditation works and so an industry has grown up around it, but you do not need to get involved. One way of keeping count is to use a mala, often made with 108 beads strung together. It saves counting but having a mala doesn't stop you from having to do the practice. You can make your own or find one online. The more you get attached to devices the harder your life becomes, even if initially they help.

Day 12 - day 14:

Keep going. Establish your own understanding of how you work. You are unique; no one is like you.

Day 15:

The third week.

This week must be about establishing your practice. Always go back to three minutes a day whenever you over extend and we all do it. Remember what you are doing. You are bringing up the problems that are stopping you get to peace. You can over complicate it but it doesn't help. You can ask others for help and they will help.In the end you are left with yourself and that is what you have to deal with.

Any bit that gets in the way is part of the dance and can be dealt with by using the Boulderstone Technique, either on your own or with a practitioner. Reaching a still point can't be compared to anything else because then it would be part of the dance.

This week is about getting to know the value of the still point. Not something that can be expressed or even something you want to express. If you get stuck and have bought a physical book bring it to my clinic and I will give you a free session. That is my promise to you. No one needs to be ill.

STILL POINT

●

Bibliography

Boulderstone, John. Living with Vitality. Findhorn Press

Davis, Roy Eugene. The Eternal Way - The Inner Meaning of the Bhagavad Gita. CSA Press

Dawkins, Richard. The Selfish Gene

Dethlefsen, Thorlsen. The Healing Power of Illness. Element

TS Eliot. Four Quartets

Hahnemann, Samuel edited by Wenda Brewster O'Reilly. Organon of the Medical Art. Birdcage Books

Hari, Johann. Lost Connections. Bloomsbury

Hay, Louise. How To Heal Your Life.

Kennedy, Robert F Jr. The Real Anthony Fauci. Children's Health Defense

Mendelson, Dr Robert. Confessions of a Medical Heretic

Patanjali's Yoga Sutras translated by John Boulderstone (unpublished)

Moskowitz, Richard, MD. Vaccines - A reappraisal. Skyhorse Publishing, Inc

Sheldrake, Rupert. The Science Delusion. Coronet

Schucman, Helen (scribe). A Course in Miracles. Foundation for Inner Peace